LIV

BEYOND

FEAR

SACRED LETTERS FROM
THE AFTERLIFE

BETH MUND AND BERIT STOVER

Creating Abundance Project, LLC

First Edition
Copyright 2019 by Beth Mund and Berit Stover

Creating Abundance Project LLC
www.thesacredletters.com

ISBN: 978-1-7340418-0-4

Printed in the United States of America

Book Design by Nu-Image
Photos by Maureen Nowak

We dedicate this book to those who helped us
believe in a world beyond fear, full of infinite possibilities.

This collection of Sacred Letters was channeled to Beth Mund and Berit Stover from the spiritual realm. The words in these letters came through to them from the voices of spirits. These Sacred Letters represent as clearly and authentically as possible the information they received and transcribed. Some of the letters are authored by recognizable names. In certain cases, the name of the author and/or the recipient of a letter has been changed to protect the privacy of the author and the family.

CONTENTS

PREFACE ix

OUR STORIES xvii

∞

Part One
OPENING THE MIND

EXPLAINING OUR MISSION

Peter 3

CELEBRATING LIFE

Deborah 9

CONNECTING WITH CONCIOUSNESS

Mariana 17

LOVING OUR SELF

Lisa Rose 23

WELCOMING CHANGE

Poppy 31

EXPRESSING OUR DIFFERENCES

Freddie 37

LOVING WITHIN THE CHAOS

Passengers From A Plane Crash 43

∞

Part Two
FEELING THROUGH THE HEART

TRANSCENDING GRIEF

Kier 51

UNDERSTANDING OUR EMOTIONS

Fiona 57

CULTIVATING FAITH
Christ Conciousness *63*
TRUSTING OUR HEART
Steven *71*
BECOMING VULNERABLE
Archangel Gabriel *79*
HEALING FROM ADDICTIONS
Peter *87*
LIVING FEARLESSLY
Grandma Ruth *95*

∞

Part Three
CONNECTING WITH ALL THERE IS

SHARING OUR SPACE
Sommer (The Dog) *101*
WALKING WITH MOTHER EARTH
Sydney *109*
HONORING THE BODY
Dawn *117*
SURRENDERING CONTROL
Frank *127*
FINDING GOD
Michael *135*
UNMASKING FEAR
Mallory *145*
MENTORING THE SOUL
Louise *153*

DEAR READER 161
QUESTIONS FOR REFLECTION 163
ACKNOWLEDGMENTS 169
ABOUT THE AUTHORS 171

PREFACE

THE STORY BEHIND THE SACRED LETTERS

Beth Mund and I are messengers. We see, hear, feel, and receive information from the spirit realm beyond our five senses. Our combined psychic abilities have opened a portal through which spiritual communication flows smoothly and rapidly, bringing us into direct contact with the souls who dictate messages in the form of Sacred Letters.

In *Living Beyond Fear*, we share twenty-one of the many channeled messages we have received from the voices of spirits in recent years. The profound insights in this collection of letters encourage us to overcome self-doubt and fear, empowering us to live a purposeful life connected with spirit and overflowing with love.

The wisdom from the world beyond the veil shared in these letters is as remarkable as the way in which these spirits came into our awareness. When Beth Mund and I first met at an intuitive training workshop in February 2016, we immediately sensed a familiarity with each other. We had both attended the session that day to gain a deeper understanding of our own spiritual path and also to make sense of the messages we had been "hearing" from people who had passed.

Receiving communication from the "other" realm was a relatively new experience for both of us, as our lives up to that point had been focused on our families and professions. While we felt the truth of the messages we intuitively received, they left us feeling surprised—in awe. A new world into the unseen realm had opened up for us, altering our perception and changing our lives as the messages began coming through more frequently and in greater detail.

When we compared the information each of us was receiving in the months that followed, Beth and I were amazed to discover that what we were receiving from spirits independently was remarkably similar. We soon realized that by working together, not only could we expand this field of awareness, but we could also bring the presence of a new spirit into the other's awareness.

This was our "Aha!" moment.

What had begun as a seemingly chance meeting was not coincidental after all. It marked the beginning of our remarkable journey together tag-teaming communications with souls in the afterlife and channeling their profound messages as transcribed letters. I received guidance in a dream that these messages were to be called "Sacred Letters" and that the collection was to be shared with others in a published book.

By deciding to combine our intuitive gifts, Beth and I expanded upon the amount of information flowing in from the beyond that we were capable of receiving by ourselves. We began to communicate with spirits in tandem, with me sensing and speaking with the spirits, and Beth recording their words with automatic writing as messages streamed through her.

By piecing together fragments of information—personality, words, images, and circumstances—we are able to bring each being more clearly into view. Beth and I collaborate daily to receive information from the souls that cross our path or that we call to us from the spiritual realm. We volley clues back and forth between one another to hone in on the spirit to know who it is and what message we are to receive.

The distinct energy from the souls who come into our awareness is undeniably present and palpable. Whether we are awoken from sleep by their visits or receive them in the midst of our daily activities, they captivate and delight us with a sense wonder. They draw us in to ponder the deeper meaning of our own lives and the mysteries beyond our understanding.

TRANSCRIBING THE MESSAGES

Beth had been writing creatively in prose and poetry for many years. One day she realized that the words, style, and flow to her writing were coming from a voice beyond her own. Although she could not identify the one speaking, she felt the distinction between her own inspired words and the words being transcribed from spirit. Whenever this happened, Beth experienced a temporary state of detachment from the physical/material world. Later, when we began to channel spirits together, she recognized that this earlier experience had prepared her to receive messages from spirits.

For me, it was not by writing but by hearing and sensing spirits that I felt their presence in a way I could no longer ignore. Earlier in my life, I had experienced visions of departed loved ones and received messages from others just as I was about to fall asleep; but it was not until recently that my ability to perceive and hear spiritual entities expanded from simple words to fuller messages.

When a letter is about to be dictated through Beth, I can sense souls waiting nearby. Some spirits simply come into our awareness; others we seek out by intuiting signs and synchronistic events. We can sense when something is asking us to pay attention to it, as if saying, "Notice this." For spirits to be heard, we have learned that they need to lower their energetic vibration and we need to raise ours.

Beth not only hears words as she writes, but she also sees the spirit or spirits in her mind's eye. With an overwhelming desire to write, propelled by a sense of powerful anticipation, Beth begins quickly translating the energy flowing through her into words on her laptop, her fingers barely keeping pace. Beth's method of channeling messages is similar to that of a court stenographer. Pages of words come through in minutes. Beth doesn't know what has been transmitted until she reads the words after the communication is complete.

Sometimes, before a Sacred Letter has been given, the spirit's identity is made clear. At other times, we work backwards and search for clues. When receiving these letters, Beth and I are often surprised at how certain souls come through, as it was not what we might have expected, given the person's age or personality when they passed. Specific references, feelings, and images let us know who is stepping forward; their words and phrases help us clarify the person to whom a letter is addressed. The spirit uses the language and/or experiences of the one channeling to convey the information of the message coming through.

Beth and I are struck by how distinct the energy of every spirit is, reflecting aspects of their personality and pieces of their soul. This helps us to distinguish between the various spirits in our midst when we want to call one of them back into our awareness to add or clarify information. Once we connect with a spirit, we have the ability to continue communication; it's as if we now have their telephone number on speed dial, and they, in turn, have ours.

These spirits have left a trail of "love letters" in hopes that our world will be lifted with their messages of love. They urge us to find our own sacred connection to our divinity and reclaim the magnificence of our shared journey in this universe.

THE COLLECTION OF SACRED LETTERS

The twenty-one unique voices in the collection of Sacred Letters in *Living Beyond Fear* include a grandparent, a yoga teacher, a young boy, a cheerleader, a dog, a famous musician, as well as the voices of those who have passed from an illness, accident, drug overdose, suicide, or natural disaster.

For each letter, we have provided an introduction to share details about the circumstances surrounding our communication with these souls. We have also offered our reflections in response to some of the letters. Beth was given the titles for the three parts of this book, along with other details, during a meditation. While these letters are addressed to certain individuals or groups, they are intended for all of us to take in, feel through, and share. The messages help us to grow in spirit, and to love ourselves and others.

These Sacred Letters have given us a profound feeling of connection in relation to both the spiritual realm and our physical plane. We continue finding ourselves as both messengers and passengers on this extraordinary journey.

The spirits in these messages urge us to open our minds, feel through our hearts, and connect with all that is. As Archangel Gabriel said in one of the Sacred Letters, "What will unfold for you, you cannot imagine. But one must try, for all we see and know is all we are capable of achieving." We sincerely thank you for joining us on this incredible journey.

Berit Stover and Beth Mund

Our use of the word "God" in this book is interchangeable with Life Force, Universe, Higher Self, Great Spirit, Creator, Source or any word you may use to describe the invisible energy of All That Is.

OUR STORIES

BETH'S STORY

The idea that we can connect with someone who has passed on, or that an "other side" actually exists, may seem like a far reach for many. I, too, was a skeptic for much of my life.

Although I was introduced to the beliefs and customs of Judaism while growing up, I never connected with the notion of an all-loving, all-powerful God. Nor did I believe in the power of prayer or an afterlife.

The journey from a skeptic to a believer in the spiritual world did not truly begin for me until confronted by the unthinkable—the birth of a stillborn child, a son, in 2004. My heart shattered, and within this deep, unimaginable abyss of grief, I came to sense a truth about life that sparked the beginning of my awareness of the afterlife.

Through a series of synchronistic events, I was referred to a grief counselor who introduced me to Brian Weiss's *Many Lives,*

Many Masters. An avid reader, I began to devour spiritual books with a hunger that could only be met by learning more about the world that lies just beyond our awareness. I studied the work of Eckhart Tolle, Joe Dispenza, Deepak Chopra, and Matt Kahn. I revisited the coursework from my MA program in psychology to make sense of and expand upon what I knew about human consciousness.

With Janet StraightArrow, I learned how to engage with spirit through shamanic journeying, which deepened my meditation practice and improved my ability to connect with my own spirit guides as well as with those who have crossed over. The world beyond my senses was becoming more familiar. With each lesson and insight, I developed greater confidence in recognizing a truth that resonated deeply—our soul lives on after death.

While opening my mind, I continued to grieve. It seemed that no amount of knowledge could minimize the emotional pain I felt or diminish my fear and anxiety. If my precious child could be taken from me in an instant, then how could any person I loved be safe? But I became aware that my illusion of control had been shattered along with my heart. In losing my son, my foundation was shaken, and in an act of trying to move beyond, I unexpectedly found solace in my love of writing.

As I expressed myself creatively, weaving words together in essays and short stories, the shattered pieces of my heart slowly began to mend. Through writing fiction, non-fiction essays, and creating a spiritually focused blog, I began to sense a higher purpose and connection as never before.

The need for control was gradually replaced with a feeling of gratitude for all I had experienced in my life. Everything in life has a purpose, even those moments that bring us to our knees. By practicing self-care, mindfulness, and learning to trust in life's meaning, I moved to a place where healing and peace could flourish. Someday, I knew I would see my son again.

There is a method to the madness that seems to occur in our lives, and if we loosen our grip and open our hearts, we will feel the truth. It is in this new space where the unexpected, even the unusual, happens. For me, messages along with an intuitive knowing began flowing from a field somewhere beyond what I could see or explain. Not long after, I began receiving dream-like images while awake, symbolic messages, and pieces of information about my own and others' lives.

Profound spiritual experiences began to occur during my meditations, including receiving the gift of a colorful healing modality, and visiting my Akashic Records, the energetic record of our souls' past, present, and potential future lives. I felt myself looking outside my body and life while seeing the roles I played. As the miraculous continued to unfold for me, synchronicities occurred daily. I slowly began to trust my intuitive knowing as an energetic source leading me down the path I was meant to follow. Its guidance was accurate, and when following this intuition, I found myself in the flow of life.

Yet, as my intuition strengthened and my gifts continued to unfold, my doubts and fears returned. I did not feel worthy of being entrusted with these insightful messages. As I wondered about these spiritual gifts, I felt as if I was being pulled back to memories from my childhood. At times, my childhood was joyous and playful, with opportunities for travel, creativity, education, and true friendship. There were moments of laughter along with wonderful memories of running through the neighborhood, climbing trees, and dancing in the living room. However, there were other instances where I experienced situations that were unsettling and frightening, creating feelings of unworthiness and pain.

Over time I began to remember what I had needed to forget. Memories of emotional and sexual abuse came into my awareness in the form of flashbacks, nightmares, and panic attacks. Picking up the discarded pieces of my past created symptoms of Post-Traumatic Stress Disorder.

Reaching beyond this additional level of intense fear meant I had to go deeper, push beyond my comfort zone as never before. To clean up this trauma required tearing off levels of denial while feeling and releasing immense anger, shame, and grief. Over time, I developed compassion for those that had made the choice to abuse rather than heal their pain.

Stopping the cycle of child abuse helped me become aware of the bigger picture of my soul and my mission. As a child, denial, daydreaming and disassociating from the physical world was a defense mechanism necessary for survival. Needing to leave my body, to protect my heart during the trauma and abuse I endured, had unknowingly created an opening within my soul for my higher self to emerge. This curious space ignited the spark of intuition that would later bring forth profound information as I developed my psychic ability to connect with the spiritual realm. I would not be me without all I had both endured and healed; for this I am grateful.

As I began to follow through in my role as a messenger, I realized that I was not the source of the information but the vessel for receiving. It was in this space where I felt deeply connected with God. I felt the truth that God was revealing my mission, what I had come here to do in this life. If God would continue healing and watching over me, I would do as guided.

All I have received in this life has been incredible. In addition to my being an empathic person guided by intuition, I have an amazing husband, who I have loved since the tender age of fourteen, and three beautiful children. I have two delightful dogs to remind me each day how precious unconditional love truly is. I am grateful for those close to me, who so openly share their love and hearts.

I know there is a heaven, or spiritual realm, just as there is a physical world. When the two connect, magic, miracles, and unconditional love unfold. If I have brought you a little piece of heaven within the pages of the Sacred Letters, then I am one step closer to fulfilling my mission to share the gifts that have been so graciously bestowed upon me.

BERIT'S STORY

Although I grew up believing in God, navigating the darkest times of my life is what deepened this relationship and opened me to receive the gifts of Spirit. We never know when those big transformative moments, the ones that awaken and shift us, are going to happen.

After graduating from college, I enjoyed a fascinating and fulfilling career as the director of a longstanding university student exchange program between Japan and the United States, and later worked in the international transportation logistics industry. My business travel crisscrossing Asia, Europe, and North America exposed me to rich cultural contrasts and perspectives while also highlighting how similar we all are at heart. During this time, I met and married my wonderful husband, and thirteen years later, our beautiful twins were born. While raising our children, I continued working as a consultant, entrepreneur, and community volunteer.

My life was blessed with great love and support from my family, friends, colleagues, and community, especially my husband and twin children. Their unconditional love and God's grace would sustain me through the unforeseen challenges and disappointments that lay ahead. I would learn the true power of this loving support in May 2010 when my life as I knew it was brought to a jarring halt.

In the five years leading up to that time, numbness and episodes of vertigo had started to occur more and more frequently. I had also been experiencing sensations of electricity, or "pins and needles," in my limbs, until one spring day, it reached a crescendo—and I lost my mobility. Upon arriving at the emergency room, my fears were confirmed. I had multiple sclerosis (MS) and lesions had formed on my brain and spine.

Although, I began getting heavy doses of steroids, I did not seem to be healing, and I lived in fear of the strange painful sensations that would surge without warning. As a mother with middle-school twins, I now had to rely completely on the support of my incredible husband, extended family, friends, and neighbors, which opened me to a deep level of appreciation and gratitude.

New fears surfaced as I began experiencing claustrophobic attacks while undergoing hours of testing encased in an MRI machine. The depressing scenarios playing out in my head got worse, along with a terrible sense of vulnerability. Although I prayed for a "do over," there was no way to get around the fear and uncertainty I was feeling. The only way forward was to accept my situation, dig deep within my being, and allow myself to feel the darkness as well as the love that surrounded me.

Lying in bed, exhausted from pushing against something that seemed immovable, I felt the overwhelming weight of it all. That was the moment when I just surrendered it all to God. I visualized my small image in God's shadow, letting go of all that I was and had hoped to be, and prayed for God to guide my family and me. While nothing had changed about my physical predicament, an extraordinary peace washed over me, filling my entire being. I sensed an incredible connection to something unseen, an expansive spiritual realm that felt so palpable and present.

This feeling reminded me of times as a young adult when I had visions of departed loved ones and sensed spirits coming to my bedside just before I slipped into unconscious slumber. Being brought to stillness with multiple sclerosis deepened my connection with God. Two messages resounded within my being: You are not alone and There is nothing to fear.

With physical therapy and time, I regained my strength and mobility. I was driving again, walking my dog Sommer, and getting the "do over" that I had hoped for. Two years passed and then in August 2012, my fourteen-year-old daughter Sarah was diagnosed with a rare cancer. Fear and uncertainty surfaced powerfully again, and yet I sensed a new strength within me. Confronting my own dark thoughts and the ongoing challenges of multiple sclerosis had prepared me to deal with my daughter's cancer. Looking back, I realize that everything in this world, the seemingly good and bad, has a purpose.

Once again, I surrendered my fears to God, knowing in my heart that although we would seek out the best medical treatment and do all we could, my daughter's life was in God's hands. Over the next difficult year, my daughter regained her health. Life resumed a sense of normalcy. To seek a better understanding of my spiritual connection with God, I enrolled in a class with Patricia Farrell, a gifted medium and spiritual teacher. Little did I know what was to unfold between Beth and me when we first met at this group in early 2016.

Patricia's guided meditations enabled me to improve the speed and accuracy of my connection with the spiritual realm. My mediumship abilities blossomed. During a guided meditation, a clapboard covered church appeared perched high on a cliff overlooking radiant blue waters. I would often return to this vision to feel and connect with many souls from the afterlife.

As my gifts continued to unfold, the brother of a group member passed away. It was then that I was given the simple image of a child's red radio flyer wagon. When I shared this with my classmate, she confirmed that a few days earlier, she and her two boys were looking at an old childhood scrapbook with photos of them riding in their beloved red wagon just moments before learning that her brother had passed. This single image seemed to open a portal where I was now able to have conversations with her deceased brother, as well as with other spirits.

Indeed, I felt like I was straddling multiple dimensions, "with one leg in the spirit world and one leg on earth," as I described it to my friend. Within hours of uttering that statement I lost all mobility in my left leg. In excruciating pain and paralyzed with the common MS symptom of a heavy-lead feeling in my leg, I was once again admitted into the hospital emergency room. I underwent extensive MRI exams on my brain and spine in an attempt to detect any sign of a MS relapse. The MRI scans showed no new lesions, leaving my doctors baffled.

Little did I know that this event would catalyze another level of awakening for my abilities as a psychic medium/messenger. While fully conscious as my flat metal bed was slid inside the MRI machine, I began to pray. At that moment, I had the most profound experience of my life. Immediately, I was enveloped in an overwhelming and indescribable feeling of unconditional love, light, and warmth. I felt the presence of Jesus and heard his words, "Peace be with you, my peace I give to you," and "I love you and you are mine."

Then, remarkably, my spirit lifted outside my body. I felt myself floating above my body, which I saw was lying on the metal bed below me, and then found myself on a grassy hillside, where I met with many spirits, standing apart from one another. I had spoken before with some of these spirits, while others were strangers. When I asked them, "What are you up to?" I became aware that all of them were engaged in one "vocation" or another in the spiritual realm.

Floating down a long portico into a vast area of brilliantly lit nothingness, I met five angels sitting at a long rectangular table upon which lay an enormous book. The Angel of Truth, who was sitting at the head of the table, with the Angels of Kindness, Patience, Compassion, and Grace sitting on either side, told me this was my Akashic Record. Before I was pulled back into consciousness, I made a solemn vow that, going forward, I would dutifully deliver every message I received, and was told that the messages I was to be entrusted with were not for me but were meant to be given to others with "great love and care."

Not long after this experience, Beth and I began to work in tandem on a daily basis, sharing and connecting with a continuous stream of spirits and angel teachers until we reached a kind of a three-way communication. I have come to believe that death is just a change of form, moving from the seen to the unseen realm. It is as though we seemingly come to an end, only to turn around and, in time, begin again.

I believe that the beauty and fullness of Heaven can be brought forth on Earth. But it will take all of us working together with a new mindset, one that recognizes our shared divinity with all of God's infinite creation. We are far more interconnected than we can imagine. We are all graced with gifts, if we only honor each other for the truth of who we are and know that each one of us is loved and worthy. Once we break free from the doubt and fear that binds us, we can create a new world with true compassion, unity, and love and the world will be made anew.

THE SACRED LETTERS

PART ONE

OPENING THE MIND

"There is so much to be felt and learned about consciousness.
We are only at the beginning."

—Mariana

PETER

Explaining Our Mission

"My dear beautiful souls, do not doubt your mission.
How it looks will unfold. You are being guided
not only by me, now, but so many."

—Peter

My cousin Peter passed in January 2017. Thirteen days later, when Beth and I had been questioning why we were receiving messages from so many different spirits, Beth felt Peter's energy. Soon after, she transcribed this extraordinary letter explaining our mission. Peter's profound words confirmed what we had thought regarding our roles as messengers guided to work together to give a "voice to the voiceless" by channeling wisdom in the Sacred Letters. Peter's letter provides insight from the other side reminding us that we are far more connected to the earth and other realms than we realize.

PETER'S LETTER (FEBRUARY 2017)

Dear Berit and Beth,

Thank you for connecting with me. I know you sensed I have been hanging around you both. I know Beth can feel my conflict. And Berit you know me in the truest sense of who I am.

Yes, I sent you a message about getting the message out. You are both more intuitive than you know. I am here to help, but first you must hear my words, learn from my lessons. It will happen in time. I am not a messenger for all, but for you both. You must teach others that there is a world from beyond; that we are not just who we think we are. That nothing is as it seems.

Where I am now, there is only love. On earth there is so much more, in order to teach, learn, and grow. But so many miss the lessons and that is where you both come in. You can teach others the gifts of pain, the wonderment in feeling uncomfortable. The beauty in reaching beyond the mirror image of the self in all it's meant to unfold and see.

You are both gifts to the world, but you just need some

help unwrapping yourselves. It is ok if the paper tears as you unfold all you are to do. Do not worry about looking neat or nice. Wrapping paper is meant to simply prolong the gift, to tantalize the ego, to make you wonder just what is inside, to pique your interest so you sit down and unwrap it and go beyond.

Sometimes, when we receive a gift from our friends or family, we love it. It is perfect and exactly what we want. And other times, well, it has missed the mark, or so we think. But it never misses the mark. There is purpose in everything. There is as much purpose in the gift we like as the one we do not. There are gifts that serve a purpose and some that simply look beautiful, opening our hearts. There are some we will use every day and some we will place upon a shelf to use less often, or at some future date.

But that is why your work is so important and needs to come out. You will be teaching others about heaven on earth, how to reach that in their lives. And to teach them that it is more than a feeling—that love—it is a state of mind. Pain and anguish, jealousy and anger are as much about unconditional love as joy and peace. When we see all as divine, as God, we let go of so much of the negativity and those shadow feelings and move into joy and bliss.

To come home to our angelic ways, we must feel our

humanness. We cannot skip it. We cannot go around it. We must go through it. Sit with all it means to be human, all life brings up for us. For mostly it arises to see if we will welcome it or push it away, sweep it under the rug. And when we welcome it without judgment, then it can go. Only when we resist it, or hide from it, does it linger.

My dear beautiful souls, do not doubt your mission. How it looks will unfold. You are being guided not only by me now, but so many. All you say and do is being guided. Where and when you go to the store or stay home. I have been guiding you both, as are many others. We take turns. This is what the Sacred Letters are about. And why you will write letters from so many of us. This is just my turn. And we will present you with who is next. But keep this task close at hand. Each day and each moment. For it is easy to get lost in the forest. As we examine the trees closely, we lose sight of their beauty.

Love to you—for now, this is all. I will return soon. Not sure if it will be me next or someone else. But always be open. You both are needed to help each other open up and let us in. And by letting us into your hearts, you will show others how to open their hearts. You have been chosen and are being guided for this mission in every moment. There are no accidents or coincidences. None. Continue to ask and all will unfold as it is guided.

Finding you in ultimate love and peace,

Peter

DEBORAH

CELEBRATING LIFE

*"When you are tempted to try and understand death,
to ask why—look at how I passed, but do not dwell on it.
Focus more on how I lived."*
— Deborah

Before cousin Peter's spirit came to clarify our mission and purpose, Beth and I had already been receiving messages and transcribing a collection of Sacred Letters. One of them was from Deborah. The circumstances through which we received her message were astonishing and chilling.

One night, Beth was startled awake by the deafening whistle of a train that seemed to be passing through her living room! Unsure that she had actually heard it and feeling a bit frightened, she cautiously searched the house for its source. It definitely sounded like a train, yet her family lived nowhere near a train track. The TV and the radio and computers were turned off, so there was no explanation for the blaring sound. It was as eerie as it was incredulous. A few minutes later, a second train whistle sounded, confirming that it was not her imagination.

Late the next evening, Beth and her husband both heard the deafening double blare of an air horn, like a train signaling as it whizzed up the tracks. Then silence. It left her husband speechless, as there was no logical explanation, and Beth pondered whether this was indeed a sign from the afterlife.

When Beth shared this story with me the next day, she said the phantom train noise could have been a way for her college friend Deborah to get her attention. Deborah had been a passenger in an Amtrak train accident. Beth asked me whether I might try to connect with her.

To feel a spirit's energy and personality, I focus on the person's first name, and then feel the nuances of the spirit stream through me as I loosely sift through the images, words, and sensations that come to me. What usually presents itself first is the person's personality. Then, instantly or over time,

I can have a conversation with the spirit talking inside my head. I was immediately struck by Deborah's strong presence, feeling so energized and uplifted by her vibrancy and zest for life. She was just bubbling with joy, telling me that she was whole, unscathed, and could still sing beautifully.

There was a familiarity about her, although I had never met her in this lifetime, and her sparkling energy remained with me throughout the day. Two days before Christmas, Deborah channeled this Sacred Letter through Beth, encouraging us to live life to the fullest. Her words, as loud and clear as that phantom train whistle, convinced us that Deborah's spirit was as alive as ever.

DEBORAH'S LETTER (DECEMBER 2016)

There you are!

Oh Joy! I am so happy to be speaking to you. I have been waiting here for the opportunity to scream out in ecstasy at where I am. I feel no pain. I feel only love. I feel so grateful to have been given such love and compassion while I was alive.

We cannot know how much time we have on this earth. It may be a few days to a hundred years. I do not have a single regret. Can you say the same?

My favorite time was with friends and family, for laughter

and love are sacred. I am so grateful and happy with the time that I had in my life, the love I received. The fun and joyous times sing out to me like Christmas cheer. I am also grateful for the time I have on the other side.

I still work, as I love to work. Can you say the same? Some of you wake in the morning and dread your day. You see your work as a punishment. But if you did not work, you would think that is a punishment, too. Some of you will lose your jobs just so you can see and appreciate working. Some of you will lose your relationships for the same reason.

It is no accident that I spent my last day supporting a friend, for that is what I loved best. Being that person who loves no matter what, speaking the truth, and letting go when it is time. Again, I must repeat myself, I have no regrets. Speak what you feel and feel it all. Be thankful for everything in your life. Hug your loved ones. Party with joy. Do not hold onto grudges. Your mistakes are not really mistakes. Your failures are not true failures. These are just detours, asking you to make a different choice, a new choice. Learn from them; do not get stuck within them.

I sense you are still thinking about how I passed. I will turn my attention there. When you are tempted to try and understand death, to ask why, look at how I passed, but do not dwell on it. Focus more on how I lived.

We all have our individual course and missions and when it is our time, we are to go. Whatever you see is meant to be. When someone marries, they are meant to marry. When someone divorces, the same is true. It does not make it fair or easy to understand. But everything is planned and you have planned it. It is our job to figure out that plan.

What is it you have come here to do? Love deeper? Laugh harder? Turn what you feel have been failures or mistakes into new possibilities. What could have been is what is. And if you don't understand it, you will. You will understand it all.

Love everything and everyone. There is no good or bad, there just is. Love death as you love life. Love sadness as you love joy. Did you know you can be in pure love and be sad at the same time? You can be in joy and feel anger? I know your mind does not think this is possible, but it is. When we are connected to our true self, our true feelings, we are in joy and love.

Allow your mind to melt away with all I say and take it into your entire being. I am bursting with energy and aliveness, yet you cannot see me and think I have disappeared. But I have gone nowhere. In fact, I am here more now than ever. I can be everywhere at once. You just need to think of me and I will be there with you.

It is no accident I came to voice myself here at Christmas time. For it is a time of rejoicing and celebration. Take this day, Christmas, and live it again and again every day—the feeling of love, light, and appreciation for all. Then there will be peace on earth. Do not sacrifice yourself, restricting what you do as an escape to not live.

Life is meant to be lived fearlessly. Immerse yourself. You never know how long you have, so live each day as if it is your last. And oh, one more thing. Don't forget to party.

Spiced eggnog is the bomb!

Deborah

REFLECTION

Beth will never forget the bold statement Deborah made in order to get her attention. Knowing Beth's skepticism, Deborah needed to "go big or go home," or Beth may not have believed it was indeed her spirit coming through. This was just how Deborah was in life —confident, outgoing, and the life of the party.

Messages from our loved ones come in all shapes and sizes, from a simple thought about them to the blaring of a train whistle running through your living room. Once you begin looking for these messages, you will realize they are everywhere.

Deborah's message still lingers, especially around Christmas time. We hope that Deborah is enjoying her eggnog and living life to the fullest.

Here's to you, Deborah!

MARIANA

CONNECTING WITH CONCIOUSNESS

"The mind is where our consciousness goes
and it can go anywhere at any time with anyone."

— Mariana

As Beth and I were finalizing our book for publication, a friend of mine alerted me about Mariana, a middle-aged woman whom I had met. She had recently suffered a brain aneurism and was left in a coma. Two weeks prior, I had received a message from my guides about people in comas. We can communicate with those in a comatose state as they are highly aware and still can hear us, despite not being able to communicate outwardly. We just need to communicate with them intuitively. I felt the truth of this, but, at the time, I didn't know anyone in a coma that I could attempt to connect with.

After learning of Mariana's situation, I felt that Beth and I could connect with Mariana despite her being miles away, lying in a hospital bed. Immediately, I saw her smile and heard her say encouragingly, "Yes, you remember me." Within minutes of sharing this with Beth, this Sacred Letter streamed through filled with gratitude.

Mariana's Letter (March 2019)

Dear Children,

Don't be fooled, silly ones. I can hear you better than I have ever heard you. My mind is no longer blocking me, telling me I am foolish or less than. Brains do in fact get in the way of higher consciousness. Talk to me. Don't let my silence fool you. I am traveling to faraway places that are right here.

My beautiful children, I am healing. You fear I am dying, but I am healing. Do not worry. I am here. Right here. There is so much about the mind we do not understand. We have studied the brain, but the mind is different. The mind is where our consciousness goes and it can go anywhere, at any time with anyone. There is no limit, or time, or space, either.

I am healing what I could not do on my own. It is like warp speed what is happening. It would take me hundreds of years to heal what this is doing in minutes. I am floating and grounded all at the same time. It is my choice to be in or out of my body. I can fly across the room like a cartoon character or spin upon my toes. I can go in and out of body. Everyone is worried, but do not worry; I am happy.

Wipe away your doubts. I have none while my body is sleeping, healing. Your doubts keep you in the box that keeps you limited. We are free but we just don't know it. We are free to speak the truth, and laugh, and heal. We are free to travel through time and space. We do not have to die or go into a coma to feel this. We can do it now. We all have the power and we have had it all along.

You don't need me to tell you this, but I will. I have sacrificed and agreed to go into this coma to heal what I need, but I am so elated to speak to you about it. To connect. To help others understand what is possible. I can hear and feel everything, like I have no skin, no coat to keep me warm. I don't need it.

Can you see me smile? I am smiling.

My memory does not fit with what I am feeling. For I am the past and future; the present is suspended in time. I am like the autistic child who knows so much but cannot voice or speak the words. He hears everything. Do not think that he does not know what is going on because he knows more than we do. He can see things we can't. He has no filter, nothing to protect him.

We focus on his emotions, as he can feel things too strongly. He feels like he is burned when we touch him, sensory overloaded, but this is because he is so open in other ways. You cannot have one without the other. At least, not yet. The human body is not designed to be that open and to also be able to have protection from another's touch. One cannot have one without the other. So stop trying to fix them and simply begin to speak their language.

A processing disorder, an emotional disorder, the autistic spectrum is simply a person so open there is no shelter, no protection. Speak his language and he will sing till his heart opens. He feels alone because he is. Nobody can understand what this feels like to feel burned by the touch. The autistic child is like I am in the coma, but I am not awake.

We have not mastered consciousness completely as humans, as we are still tied to the brain and it's keeping us in the dark, so to speak. There is so much we don't know and so much more to know. If you stop asking the questions, you will not find the answers. Continue opening yourself up as humans and moving beyond the conscious mind. Do not let your jaw drop in awe when someone connects with someone's spirit who has passed, but do it yourself and know it to be the truth. Stop denying. Stop the skepticism and you will begin to open. It can be the hard way, with a crow bar, or come easily if you set the time aside to connect with your higher self, to move past your mind.

Learn from those who are here—the autistic child or those that have had a near death experience. Learn from a stroke victim and what they feel, how consciousness feels. Move past the confines of the mind and open the box we have all climbed into. There is so much to be felt and learned about consciousness. We are only at the beginning. Do not wait. Do not be afraid to speak about it. Do not look to those that are special or without a voice and think they have nothing to say, to add. They have more to say than you know.

Know this is coming from me so that you can begin to open your mind and climb out of that box. Stop trying to plan and restrict. Open up your mind and your calendar. Allow your days to unfold instead of planning them all. And listen to those whose voice we cannot hear through normal channels.

Those who are open are healing with energy. Those who are open know healing with energy is possible. Those who are open can do what we see as a miracle. The future will bring healing centers, replacing our hospitals. We have no idea what the body is capable of; we have no idea what we can do for each other.

We are so limited and captured like prisoners here on this earth, bumping into one another, blaming and taking things out on each other. What we really want to do is become free. Follow our knowing and reach for what we think is unobtainable. Do not be afraid to speak out what you know. I have no voice at the moment and it can feel like a prison. So thank you for receiving mine.

You have a voice. Use it. Break free and use it. And help to bring forth these messages for those that think they are too afraid, broken, or damaged to use their voice. Listen to the meekest of voices for what they need to say—they often come through with the most powerful of messages. Follow your dream and release fear or doubt.

Thank you for receiving me today. Thank you. Thank you. Thank you. Thank you.

Mariana

LISA ROSE

LOVING OUR SELF

*"Get to know yourself outside of what others think of you.
Inside each of your hearts is a beautiful castle
of unconditional love."*

— Lisa Rose

One frigid winter night in our town, two high school seniors were driving home from cheerleading practice when their car hit an icy patch and slammed into an oncoming vehicle. One of the girls passed instantly; the other died later that night at the hospital. The community was numb with grief, as the hopes and dreams of two beautiful girls were gone.

Years later, at my daughter's high school memorial scholarship ceremony, I was reminded of Lisa Rose, one of the cheerleaders, and immediately felt her presence. Although I had not known her, the images and sensations that surfaced within me clearly signaled that it was Lisa Rose.

She entered my visual field like a giant sunburst, radiating light outward. While her energy felt luminous and expansive, I was keenly aware that she was quietly observing all the emotions and actions of the young people in that full auditorium. I shared with Beth that Lisa Rose's demeanor felt caring and without judgment. I learned that she had been a flyer on the school's cheerleading squad. Now she seemed to have a bird's-eye view from her spiritual vantage point of both the seen and unseen worlds.

She was laid to rest in a hillside cemetery overlooking her beloved high school. It is in an area that Beth drives past several times a day. One day, to Beth's surprise, her young son Drew asked her to turn down the cemetery road on their way home from school. He wanted to look at the names on the gravestones. Moments after walking into the cemetery, Drew called Beth over to see what he'd found. The name on the gravestone in front of them was "Lisa Rose." Beth smiled, feeling the genuine beauty of this girl, inside and out. She gazed across the hill to the high school in the distance, the school for which Lisa Rose had cheered.

Lisa Rose's spirit seemed focused on young people, as we

could especially feel and hear her when Beth and I were offering support to our teen-aged children and their friends. One afternoon, while Beth's daughter and her friends were gathered at her home to discuss the trials and tribulations of high school, Lisa Rose's words of wisdom came through in this Sacred Letter.

LISA ROSE'S LETTER (NOVEMBER 2017)

Dear Classmates:

We navigate and prepare for so much in life, except for those instances that are in our blind spots—those we never think will happen. Throughout our lives, especially during our teens, we often feel invincible. We do not think about the unthinkable and believe we are safe from tragedy and loss.

We never know how much time we have. Like the morning frost that melts as the sun warms the air, appreciate and drink in the beauty of what is in front of you, for it is fleeting. And as the moments turn into minutes, hours, days, and years, drink in everything you see, hear, taste, and touch as if it is your last moment.

Creating a wonderful life comes from a place of love. And there is nothing more loving than building each other up. Reach out and allow your hand to linger in case another is having a hard time. We are all in this together. There is no pressure for you to get this. I only ask that you take in my words and let them seep slowly beneath your skin, where your heart knows the truth of them.

You all have strength within you to be yourself. Your changing bodies, stress of school, social media, grades, sports, and pressure from society have created this wedge between your true self and the person you show up as. There is nothing more beautiful than being yourself. You are unique and you matter. You are perfect as you were created. Your body, your hair, your face, your strengths and weaknesses are all a part of you and meant to be. The greatest gift you can give the world is to be yourself. Life can become confusing when we believe we are supposed to be different than we are. It is confusing because it is not the truth.

Life is not about who is the prettiest, the smartest, or the coolest. Fleeting moments of attention have nothing to do with self-worth or who any of you are deep down. In fact, they wind up creating more distance between your heart and head.

Get to know yourself. Know how amazing you are from the inside out. Put down your phones and pick up your heads to see how incredible our world is, how beautiful words can sound to another when giving a compliment. Get to know yourself outside of what others think of you. Inside each of your hearts is a beautiful castle of unconditional love. Take care to notice what is in your moat around your castle. Is it filled with kindness, compassion, and your true self or competitive social media posts that do not reflect your best thoughts?

Our words matter. Our actions matter. We all matter.

It is never too late to make a difference for yourself. And when you see someone acting blindly from hatred, why not say no? Not today. Not on my watch.

As a cheerleader, I flew through the air, always grateful and trusting that I would be caught by those standing beneath me with open arms. Some of you are at the bottom of the pyramid because your job is to steady and balance others, and some of you are reaching for the stars, being lifted and guided. Neither is worse or better, but each of us has a role based on our strengths and gifts. Be strong in your conviction, no matter your job and know the beauty of the pyramid is to have balance and work together as a team. Life is about unity and cooperation.

Become a flyer or take to your knees as a base. Just don't forget to look to the left and right and see who is by your side. There are no mistakes as to who is working alongside you. And when you remember, pay them a compliment; lift them up. For next time, it may just be you that needs it in that moment.

Life is about moments. Life is about learning. Life is about opening our hearts so that another can open theirs. Lift each other up, so when we all fall, we are all held safely beneath the parachute of each other's love. Stop and take notice. And you will be supporting the soul.

Lisa Rose

REFLECTION

Lisa Rose expressed her relief and gratitude that Beth had the gift to be able to put her message on paper. She seemed to have looked through Beth's eyes that winter day as Beth was watching the frost shimmer in the sunlight on the grassy field behind her home.

When we shared Lisa Rose's letter with her parents, her mother responded that yes, her seventeen-year-old daughter had been a cheerleader, but only for her last two and a half years. She spoke of Lisa Rose's other interests and talents; she was an accomplished gymnast as well as a gifted artist who created beautiful, delicate drawings. She shared how Lisa Rose loved to laugh and be silly with her friends, and that she was looking forward to graduating from high school to begin the next phase of her life.

The response of Lisa Rose's mother was an important reminder that when a spirit comes through to channel a specific message in their Sacred Letter, one may be surprised as to what is shared. There is often a higher meaning and purpose to the insights that are revealed symbolically from this other realm.

POPPY

WELCOMING CHANGE

*"To welcome change, one must cultivate the courage
to feel safe enough to take risks."*

— Poppy

Beth's father-in-law died from complications of pneumonia. Poppy's spirit first came through to Beth one night when she had invited a spiritual teacher, a psychic medium, to her home for a private session with a group of friends. Although skeptical, and having no experience with mediums, something urged Beth's husband to join the small group.

Almost immediately, Poppy's voice came through the medium to offer business advice about an investment that Beth's husband was considering. Throughout his life, Poppy had always given his son business advice; he was continuing to do so from the afterlife.

Not long after that evening, I too would begin to feel Poppy's presence. While sitting reading a newspaper at the hair salon or walking down the aisles of the grocery store, he would give me messages for people. Poppy's energy was quiet, caring, and steady, as if he wanted to empower those around him. The image that came to me was of Poppy steering a sailboat downstream, and then, with a smile, giving the wheel to someone else, fully confident in their ability to read the winds. Yes, you might make mistakes, but his belief in you was unwavering.

Still very present, guiding and supporting his loved ones, he dictated this Sacred Letter to Beth for her husband, Poppy's beloved son. This message about change and stepping into our highest self is intended for all of us.

Poppy's Letter (December 2016)

Dear Son,

Words cannot express how proud I am of you and how much I love you. You are the brightest soul in a sometimes dark world. You are incredible and worthy of the greatest life. Put your hand on the stick shift and drive that Maserati into the sunset because you want to. Release the "should" and become honest with all you desire.

Change is inevitable. It is happening all around you. It is happening to you and everyone at such a rapid pace. I know you feel as if you cannot catch your breath. There is nothing to be afraid of with change. When we resist change, fear and stagnation arise. I know that change can be scary. The secret is, we are never in control. Life can be overwhelming when you try and do it all yourself.

Welcoming change takes both faith and courage. Have faith, as you are never alone. You are loved beyond this world and while you may feel at times like your task is insurmountable, it is because you feel you must do it alone. But I am here, as are so many others who love you. I have faith in all you are here to do and be.

It is simple, but very often our minds complicate things. Our minds perceive many obstacles blocking us from moving forward on our life's path. We may even view new things as threatening to take from us what we have worked so hard to obtain, instead of trusting in life's flow.

Sometimes I know you feel as if you cannot breathe, the stress pressing down upon your chest. But if you slow down, and trust, you will see how much you are cared for. You will understand and feel the love and compassion encircling you and opening new changes within you and your life with such ease and grace.

You are not alone in your fears. Many only go so far in trusting or taking risks before running back to where they feel safest. Like standing on a high diving board and staring down at the water, wondering when the best time would be to jump. What many do not realize is that retreating and descending down the ladder will be more painful than if they take the plunge. The more we wait, succumb to fear, the more pain we feel.

To welcome change, one must cultivate the courage to feel safe enough to take risks. This comes from opening our hearts up to receiving love. I feel the need to tell you, again, that you are so loved; but I know you question this often. Yet if you look around you each day at those who care about you, you will see the love.

Reach beyond what you know, and you will see that you will always be taken care of, no matter what. Regardless the height of the diving board, know that you will hit the water perfectly and find yourself swimming within the waters of love with all those around keeping you afloat. This will feel magnificent.

Release all resistance to change by remembering that you

are loved, cared for, and worthy of everything that comes forth in your life. That is the key.

I love you and I am here to help. Trust yourself. Trust your loved ones. Trust in a higher being. I am here surrounding you with the highest love imaginable. Open your eyes and feel with your heart. You will find it easier to surrender to what will be by going through your days without worry or fear of what is around the corner. You will feel safe, and cared for, and able to take risks outside your comfort zone.

That is part of it—working through the discomfort. Just beyond this zone is everything you have ever imagined possible; everything you have ever wanted. A life filled with the most incredible joy, love, and peace. Change is inevitable; I see so many ready to hold your hand along the way.

Trust in the flow of life. It is here to take you to the most magnificent of places. Stay for a moment, or as long as you can, within this space. Over time, you will find your heart will begin to feel worthiness, love, abundance. Beauty, like you never imagined.

A whole new world is waiting for you to reach out and grab it. Are you ready? We believe in you.

Today is the best day to start anew.

You are loved.

Poppy

REFLECTION

Beth smiled, knowing that Poppy's unconditional love for his son had not ended with his passing. She felt his warmth and pride, honoring his son for all that he was doing for his family and others. Beth told me how lucky she felt to have known her loving father-in-law, who had stood as her husband's best man at their wedding.

Upon receiving this message, Beth's husband did not immediately respond, but wanted to ponder it for a while. Later that day, he texted Beth a funny cartoon about change that had come through his social media feed. A caterpillar was sitting across the table from a butterfly. "You've changed," remarks the caterpillar. "We are supposed to," says the butterfly.

FREDDIE

EXPRESSING OUR DIFFERENCES

"Know I succeeded, not through my music, but in being me."

— Freddie

The synchronicities in our lives leave Beth and I marveling at how seemingly unrelated events bring these spirits and their Sacred Letters into our awareness. It reaffirms for us that nothing is a coincidence.

I had been guided to watch a video about transgender youth on Vice on HBO and was struck by the words of a five-year-old girl. While playing with her princess toys, she casually remarked to the interviewer that she had had to wait until she could speak before she could tell her mommy that she really was a girl, despite being born a boy. I shared with Beth that I felt a letter waiting to be channeled, honoring our personal identity.

The following morning, Beth felt guided to scan the movies playing at the local theater. Immediately, it became clear that she was to see the 2018 movie *Bohemian Rhapsody*, celebrating the life of musical icon Freddie Mercury. As Freddie's life unfolded on the big screen, Beth felt him deep within—his triumph as well as his struggle to stay true to who he had always felt himself to be.

After she saw the film, Beth told me she felt his quirky and light-hearted energy lingering, encouraging her to play, dance, and feel his music. Days passed and suddenly a video about Freddie Mercury came onto her laptop screen and the music seeped into her being. Within moments, Freddie delivered this powerful Sacred Letter about embracing our differences and honoring our individuality. Although Freddie addressed this message directly to the LGQBT community, his poignant words are important for all of us to hear.

FREDDIE'S LETTER (NOVEMBER 2018)

Dear LGQBT Community:

The show must go on, darling. Do not get caught up in what you are not. Reach for the possibilities and do not worry about where your feet land. We are all created beautifully in God's eyes. We are all meant to be exactly who we were born to be.

Follow your knowing, for there is a world of gifts waiting for you. Unfold your hands. Empty your mind. Open your heart and let it in. Look beyond what is not yet known, the seemingly impossible. Do that. Do it with the fierceness of a thousand lions racing across the plains. Do it like your last meal depends upon it. Do not look to your left and right. Do not look behind, but ahead. Release the pressure to be the same, to be like your neighbor. No, do not do as others have done. Do as you are meant.

Our differences are like Joseph's multi-colored coat. He is not special. We all have the colorful coat we show to the world. But inside we are all the same. We are all One. I am not better than anyone else, I just could not ignore my gift. It was literally in my face. God made it that way or I may not have done what I came here to do — touch you with what was within my heart. Had I been less unique, I may not have been able to pull you along with me to help you open up and see that even the darkest places have endless possibilities of light.

Look at your body, your outside, and see where you are different. That is where your gift is. Do not look at it as a problem or ugly. This is a clue: how you are different will be the key to how you can make a change in the world, in your world. Expand upon this different way about you. Perhaps it is the way you speak or how you look? Maybe one area is too big, another too small? Too wide or too many? This is the way in; this is the key.

You were made this way so you could expand upon your differences to bring forth your gifts. Find those gifts. Share those gifts. Scream out those gifts. How you are different is how you can change the world. Find that fashion that makes your heart sing. Name your uniqueness. Call attention to yourself in the most unique way possible. Do not look to others who have failed but follow me. Know I succeeded, not only though my music, but in being me.

Dress up your outside to match your inside, who you are, and know that is how it is meant to be done. Do not adhere to the current climate or custom. For that is boring. Plain. Mundane. We have too many of those, not enough of these. It is far too easy to let those in charge tell you who to be. Be yourself and you will not be swayed away from who you are meant to become. Push through the status quo and break out into a brand new life, a miraculous you.

Be aware of those looking to keep you small for their needs. Break through to the other side of you, of life, of love. Burst apart that bubble that keeps who you are away from the world. We need you; we need your uniqueness, your difference, your passions, and your heart. We need your look and your fashion. We need more that are different, not ones that are the same.

We can all sing with the music, our performances limited between birth and death. We are all on one big stage and the more we interact, the greater the energy between us. When we sing together, we can rise up against any oppression of our differences. It does not matter what is real life or fantasy. It is all illusion and all real. It is one big mind fuck. Isn't it glorious, my dear? How fun! We all need to have more fun.

Our feelings; sometimes, they are all we have to push us higher in this life. Don't be boring. Don't adhere to the status quo. Rise above. Become the black sheep. The white sheep need you to speak for them, raise them up to where they cannot go. Perhaps our dreams are real and our reality is a dream. Wouldn't that be nice? Wouldn't it be grand to break down those that break us? Dress them in different attire so that they too may see you and they too can become someone else. And that someone else is exactly who they are meant to be when they take off their outdated ways, their traditions, and allow their true self to break through.

Each has their lessons, and mine was to put it in their face. That is what I was meant to do—put who I am in your face, while getting beneath your skin. Making you feel the energy, the connection of our spirit. The fascination with my lifestyle was because you could not do that yourself—become something different. Grow beyond your roots. They looked to me to pull off my petals, one by one.

For you want a piece of me to become fully you. You want to break out of the mold. You can do it. Break away from those that hurt you, keep you small. Break open the person you are meant to be. Break apart those silly rules of who we are supposed to be as humans, as people. There are no rules about how to dress, how to look, how to wear your heart on your sleeve. Be the champion of your own life. Put aside what others think, they are just bogged down by what they cannot be.

You can do anything. You can be anything. You can start now.

We put musicians on pedestals, for they speak the words we long to say but cannot. They dress, behave, and do as they please. Know that you think you need us, but you don't. You can be the champion of your own heart, your own life. We are all champions, my friend.

Nothing really matters.

Nothing really matters to me.

Freddie

PASSENGERS FROM
A PLANE CRASH

LOVING WITHIN THE CHAOS

*"Loving within the chaos happens one heart at a time.
Start with your own, and then slowly, one by one,
share your love with another."*

— Passengers from a Plane Crash

One day, I shared with Beth that I was aware of a crowd of spirits standing on the left stage of my visual field. This was not unusual, since Beth and I often have many spirits waiting to speak to us. To serve the spirits that come in, we have installed an imaginary ticket machine to dispense numbers; a large decorative one in turquoise and orange, similar to what you might use when you get in line to place your order at a deli. What was different on this particular morning was that I sensed an enormous group standing behind Number One. They were all holding airplane tickets and were the passengers from a plane crash. As they stepped forward to speak with me, I felt their presence but was unable to hear their voices.

While sharing this information with Beth, she saw them showing her the image of a radio dial. They indicated that with one slight adjustment on my part, I could move into their vibrational frequency. Beth then described them handing me two books, one with Edgar Poe's short story, "Eleonora," and a book on translation.

Then I saw them move as One to center stage. Beth shared that a Sacred Letter had flowed through her within minutes that day.

PASSENGERS FROM A PLANE CRASH LETTER (JUNE 2016)

To all souls living through the darkness:

There is a tendency to look outside of ourselves to see how we have progressed, to look to others for their approval and opinions. But when we do that, we lose our ability to come into our own knowing and power. This is also true if we look upon the world to see how evolved our world has become.

Looking out upon the world, we can see chaos, turmoil, hatred, and fighting. We turn on the news and see mass shootings, out of control fires, and constant fighting within the political arena. We are not denying all that is happening. It is right there in front of us each and every day. It is across the world, and right next door.

The worst of the darkness comes just before the light dawns. Can you seek out the peace, joy, and love that are hidden within the chaos? We need to look for the pockets of light that are spreading throughout the world. Look for these pockets rising up from the ashes. It is these pockets of space that we need to fill with love.

Spreading love is your mission. It is all of our mission. How do we best fill up these pockets of space with love? We need to ask, and wait for an answer. When Mother Teresa travelled the world, feeding the poor and hungry, she did not look for those she could not reach, but followed her mission guided by her heart, and walked her path. The reason we become lost and do not know our mission is because our vision has clouded over from looking at the world and seeing how overwhelmingly chaotic it has become.

We must become aware of what can get in the way of our mission of spreading love. Beliefs of fear, doubt, worry, lack—these are illusions and we must not let them get in our way of loving within the chaos and finding those pockets. When our minds go to what we cannot change, we must understand this is interference. We must discard these thoughts, as they are part of the darkness and do not help us in any way. Believe that you can see past the obscurity, and you will. It is not just in the moments that we can see change, but in the hours, days, and years.

We must love within the darkness, as if we are blind and cannot see all we are doing to help. Change takes time, and it will become obvious as goodness spreads. Until that time, the more you see goodness, the more goodness you will see.

Loving within the chaos happens one heart at a time. Start with your own, and then slowly, one by one, share your love with another. This will open their heart, and we will be on our way to changing our world once and for all.

Our passing as we did was a message that our planet was in danger of becoming more explosive and violent, and we needed to take note of a growing sect of individuals whose acts of terror would grow in size and scale. Terrorism does not grow overnight. It is a result of longstanding circumstances of neglect, feelings of separation, and hopelessness. If we can continue as a country to open our eyes, hearts, and minds to those lost in the darkness, we can all begin to feel the love and light without destroying another. That is our right and freedom as humans—to love, welcome the light, and help those most lost within the darkness.

The terror that occurs today continues to come forth from the darkness, and in its aftermath, one can see the compassion and love that pours out to those most affected, those left behind by the horrific departure of their loved ones so seemingly mercilessly without sense. We must seek out ways for preventing future acts of terror.

Within each act of terror, a light is born in its aftermath. It is the space where the heart is most open. If we can, we need to look for the love in times of peace and quiet, and pray for the need for terror to diminish, as well as reach out to those suffering in the depths of separation and pain, so all acts of terror eventually become extinct from our world. Watch the goodness that erupts with each act of terror, and the unity that rises up against a few misguided souls, and ask for this light to stay with us, overcoming and pushing out the next act of terror now and forever.

Yes, our world looks chaotic. We must look for the peace. Yes, our world looks dark. We must see the light. Yes, our world looks dangerous. We must search out our safety. And we must open our eyes to what we see at each moment, and no matter what, open our hearts to love.

Find your strength and carry on. And spread your love. After all, it is our mission shared by one and all.

Passengers from a Plane Crash

REFLECTION

The images mirrored Poe's own story of going from joy to sorrow following the death of his beloved cousin Eleanora. It reminded me of what other spirits have said—that the amount of light we choose to see in our world colors our reality. Seeking light, even in the darkest of places, will bring new light.

Beth and I both remarked on how important this message is in today's world, where we are constantly bombarded by news with scenes of terror and chaos, spreading fear in communities across the globe. Yet, we also see many people quietly radiating their light. We create ripple effects with our words, actions, and thoughts.

As the American spiritual teacher Ram Dass once said, "We are all just walking each other home." We are all in this together. By being present for each other and listening attentively, we affirm and celebrate our humanness. Together, we can move beyond the chaos to create a new reality reflecting our shared divinity.

PART TWO

FEELING THROUGH
THE HEART

*"Life is a mix of joy and pain, both needed to create
the space for tears and laughter to fall together in harmony."*
—Kier

KIER

TRANSCENDING GRIEF

"Find a way to go on each day, to survive the grief,
until that one day when you begin living again. And then know,
feeling joy once again—this is how I want you to be."

— Kier

I will always remember my cousin Kier for his gentle, thoughtful ways, and his sense of wonder and curiosity. Whenever he shared a new discovery with me, his deep-blue eyes sparkled, and a smile lit up his face. As a child, he was fascinated with geography and faraway places, often poring over the colorful maps and geographic formations pictured in the enormous "Great Atlas" that sat on a table in our grandparents' home. Later, he would live in Japan, captivated by the beauty of its land, language, and people, before returning to California to work as a geospatial analyst in Silicon Valley.

Sadly, when I reconnected with Kier, he was in a hospital bed, diagnosed with a rare sarcoma cancer; a metastatic tumor had ruptured his intestine, adding a painful new complication after months of chemotherapy and surgeries. During my time with him, I shared what Beth and I were receiving on his behalf from the angelic realm. Kier would smile as he pondered the messages. There was an incredible grace about him.

Kier passed the following month, surrounded by family and loved ones, and channeled several letters to us, including penning his own eulogy, within days of his passing. I read this Sacred Letter at his memorial service on March 3, 2017 to the family and friends gathered in the Japanese teahouse overlooking the beauty and tranquility of the Zen gardens at Hakone Estate in Saratoga, California.

KIER'S LETTER (MARCH 2017)

To my family and friends:

I am honored and humbled by your presence today on what could be a somber day, filled with sadness and grief. But I ask you a favor today. I ask you to look upon what I have experienced and will continue to experience with honor and grace. As you had to bear witness to both the wonder of life and the cruelty of death, always remember that I have been given the greatest gift in living upon this earth. It is not quantity but quality that matters. For one can live to be a hundred and have opened another's heart, but only once. Or one can live one year and open the hearts of hundreds.

While you may miss that you can no longer touch or see me how you are used to seeing me, I am still here. I can be felt and known in a different way, a way that looks beyond the physical. Look around you now. You cannot see me with your eyes, but I am with you right now, as I have never left. My breath continued on into the afterlife. I can be felt right beside you, holding you, hugging away your pain, and high above, showering harmony and love down upon all of you.

Don't be fooled by the physicality of everyday life. Look beyond. Look within. And you will find me joining you by your side. I will be playing with my son, lying on the floor beside his toys. With you, I will be walking the grocery aisles choosing foods, riding in the back seat of the car enjoying the passing scenery and hopping aboard a jet plane on an adventure. I will be within and throughout all the wondrous pleasures of life.

Please join me. Discard your umbrella and feel the coolness of rain upon your skin, and the warmth that emerges with the rising sun. Forget your shoes and dance upon the grass with bare feet. Can you do that? Can you live each day like you are dying, like it is your last? Can you have no regrets living life as it is meant to be lived, in love, harmony, and beauty?

We are all here for a reason and what better gift can I give you today than to encourage you to follow your heart, align with your soul, and hop aboard the train before it leaves the station. Ask yourself today, what am I to do today to open my heart to share a whisper or lend a hand? Push yourselves beyond your comfort zone. Ask yourself the hardest questions about life, love, and what is beyond, and then listen. Listen day and night, hour by hour, moment to moment. The answers will come in many different forms, but they will come. Messages will be given that I am alive and well. They will come in the flutter of a butterfly's wing, the sparkle in a child's eye, the reminder of pain. Yes, even pain. For life is a mix of joy and pain, both needed to create the space for tears and laughter to fall together in harmony.

While it is unheard of to speak at your own funeral, what better time than now to start breaking with tradition? While tradition is good, do not take customs and beliefs to your grave. Ideas are meant to change, grow, and intersect with life. Allow the serenity of daily routines to be melded with the joy of curiosity and surrender to God. God is everywhere. We are One. We are love.

To my friends and family who loved and nurtured me through both hardship and ease, I am forever grateful. Even in my darkest hour, I did not regret one moment of my life. I love you more than I can even put into words. You were and continue to be my world. Find a way to go on each day, to survive the grief, until that one day when you begin living again. And then know, feeling joy once again—this is how I want you to be. For you may feel torn, to not want to forget me, and dwell endlessly in sadness. But know this is not how I need you to remember me. It is in your joy each day that I will be filled up with unconditional love. And I will hand this love right back to you, now and forever. And we will be tied eternally in a circle of love, joy, and remembrance.

Smile when you think of me.

I have never left.

I am here always.

All my heart,

Kier

FIONA

UNDERSTANDING OUR EMOTIONS

"Like me, you have a profound moral compass inside of you to speak the truth in every moment."

— Fiona

It still astonishes us when a Sacred Letter streams through and seemingly disparate clues begin to fit together; often their meaning only becomes clear to us later on. That was the case when receiving this message for Emma, an American college student, from the spirit of Fiona, a young Liberian teen who passed in the Ebola epidemic in Monrovia, Liberia, in 2014. I had felt Fiona's presence after hearing "More Than Me" founder Katie Meyler pay tribute to Fiona in a speech on the epidemic at the Women's

International Forum held at the United Nations in 2015.

Katie described Fiona walking into Monrovia's quarantine center surrounded by medical staff, unrecognizable in their head-to-toe protective white moon-suits. Fiona was clutching a pink stuffed animal and disposable cell phone, both gifts from More Than Me.

Sadly, Fiona never went home

Two years later, I came across a letter that Katie had posted on the More Than Me website in memory of Fiona. I shared Fiona's photo with Beth. In the picture, this young girl was sitting alone in the back of one of the ambulances the charity had donated to respond to the Liberian crisis.

Now, upon reading this tribute, I once again sensed this young girl standing quietly in the left wing of my visual stage. I could feel Fiona's pensive energy and her thoughts of her mother. She was honoring her mother, knowing that while her mother could not hold Fiona's hand, she held her in her heart, as Fiona did her mother. There was strength within Fiona and a worldliness that prompted her to share her wisdom.

She came center stage to channel a letter just after Beth had been talking with a college student who was feeling anxious and uncertain. It was as if Fiona from Liberia had overheard the conversation and was now offering her wisdom from the spiritual realm to help this American girl realize her inner strength. Though these two girls were from opposite sides of the globe and from very different cultures, they shared a deep connection.

Fiona's Letter (January 2017)

Dear Emma,

You have been given a gift. It is called strength. Many times, when we are strong, we don't know how powerful we are. This power can enable you to offer advice, helping others so matter-of-factly that you may forget how your words are to be delivered so that they are truly heard. We do not mean to hurt others. So often this happens when we are not paying attention; for example, if we absent-mindedly open an envelope, we can slice open the skin, getting a paper cut.

Your intentions are in the right place, but words that come out full of strength can sometimes be overpowering and get lost. If you can soften your strength and round out the edges when speaking with others, you will be heard so much more! You have such incredible advice, words of profound wisdom—I want others to be able to hear you. Make no mistake, this strength is a gift. I want you to know that. I have learned that.

Many do not know how to soften their strength. How

do we do that? We soften our strength with feeling. When we are strong and show our strength first, we can often be labeled as unfeeling and unaffected by much of what is happening around us. But we both know that is not the truth—for you or me. We have both put our feelings on hold when faced with hard times. We just need to find them and bring them back to the surface. You and I, and the many who hide their feelings, often feel hurt and pain just as strongly as those who wear their heart on their sleeve.

What you agreed to before coming into this life was to incorporate this strength on all levels, making it a part of your entire being. No matter what we endure in this life, we must use all our strength to keep us close to wholeness as much as possible. And we must not allow this strength to hide the side of us that remains most vulnerable. To feel is to show the most valuable lesson of strength. That is what wholeness is about.

We have come from such different backgrounds, you and I, such different upbringings, that it seems strange for us to be talking. But deep down, we are the same. What costume we wear during our lifetimes does not change who we are deep down. We have the same fears. I know you, as I know myself. You fear that if you open up just a bit to your feelings, the pipes will burst open, but this rarely occurs. Our pipes only burst open when closed off for good. There is no place for our emotions to escape and this is when they burst, leaving us in pieces.

Please know that by showing this vulnerability, you will not lose your edge. In this past life, I was quarantined from everyone because of disease; I was physically cast aside. I tell you this because so many also do this emotionally. Wall themselves off, as if on an island, and this prevents others from reaching us, knowing us, touching us. And us, from affecting them as well. This is such a lonely place to be. This was such a profound lesson for me to not be able to be physically near anyone that I am hoping to teach others not to do this with their hearts. My wish for you is to let others in—without worry of being hurt.

Open yourself up to love, friendship, and feelings. We both know who you are deep down, how much you really feel. You will help others so much if you share your truest self, how you feel, with others. You are a wise and knowing girl. Showing your vulnerability, along with your strength, will help you to move mountains.

You are learning at the moment and doing an amazing job. We could not ask for a better teacher for those around you. You are teaching the importance of loyalty and friendship, as well as how wasteful it is to become shallow, mistaking one's appearance alone for beauty. This is who you are and it is beautiful. Show that to the world!

Like me, you have a profound moral compass inside of you to speak the truth in every moment. This will continue to serve you as you move on in your life and mission. And as you let the emotional piece begin to drip from you, you will be that much more effective in reaching others with the truth. It is like honing your skills, sharpening the knife, and then learning how far to puncture the skin. To allow the wound to be felt, but not to the point that someone bleeds out, for that would prevent them from getting the teaching, and the lesson will go unnoticed.

I know you do not know why you are here, or think you don't care right now, but we did this to make your experience on earth that much more powerful. While the roles we play are temporary, the lessons are ongoing. It is not the masks we wear or parts we play in our lives that matter, but how much we affect one another.

You have been put in the perfect place and time to help bring our world back into alignment and purpose.

Your journey is vast and your leadership strong. All is not what it appears to be. You are a diamond in the rough. Now it is time to let you shine!

Much love and light, beloved being.

Fiona

CHRIST CONCIOUSNESS

CULTIVATING FAITH

"We must rest in the awareness that there is always a gift in everything, even if we cannot see it."

— Christ Consciousness

Beth and I had enrolled in a course called, "Moving into the Heart of Love." A small group of us came together in this online class to identify the limitations that prevent us from expressing the love that we are. This course brought our attention to our own personal obstacles to work through. We were told that a boulder-like challenge would be revealed to each of us in the coming weeks.

Shortly after this prophecy, Beth received a text message from Alicia, one of the participants, asking for guidance. Things were spiraling downward for this young mother, who lived miles away and was suffering from emotional stress after the loss of a long-term relationship. Serious physical issues further complicated an already difficult situation. Without health insurance and unable to work, her financial debts mounted. She wondered whether she had done something to bring on such hardship.

Life is not predictable, nor is it easy to navigate. We question why things happen. Many of us ask, Why do bad things happen to good people? When things begin to fall apart, and while in the midst of great challenges and tragedies, some people wonder, where is God? Where is the love to support and carry us in the darkest of times? Why do we go through such hardships?

As if in response to these questions, a spirit embodying Christ Consciousness, steadfast in its faith and unshakable in its love, came through with this Sacred Letter.

CHRIST CONSCIOUSNESS LETTER
(DECEMBER 2016)

Dear Alicia,

It is a hard time for all. We know all that you are asking and praying for. We hear you. We are not withholding to punish you. You have done nothing wrong. You have endured and continue to endure great hardship, but you are stronger than you know.

Nothing is harder than to feel like we are alone and our prayers are going unanswered. But you must forgo doubt for trust. You must have faith that you are being heard, and although we can have a timeline as humans for when we should feel better or how our prayers should be answered, this may not be the way our journey is to unfold.

We can pray for what we think we need, but we must put our personal agendas aside and know in our hearts we will receive all that we need. Every prayer is heard; every prayer is answered. It is not by the outcome that we can be sure that we are heard, but in our ability to trust in our hearts that there is a reason why we have been brought to our knees.

Sometimes there is a bigger gift when we do not get what we want. For what God may give us is always for our highest path, even if it makes us uncomfortable. We must rest in the awareness that there is always a gift in everything, even if we cannot see it. And we must release our attachment to outcome in order to receive our answers in the highest form, knowing that we are always cared for.

We could simply request: "Let all that I need come to me today. Please make itself known in the exact moment I am meant to know it. And please allow me not to dictate how God is there for me. Give me strength so that I can contin-ue to trust that I am deeply loved, and that God is always following the most incredible plan. Help me to remain open to God's plan and all will make itself known to me in time."

To release our personal agenda and will is to truly surrender to God and love. Learning patience is just as important as getting back on our feet financially—even more so. To have faith in the circumstances is to know that we are always in God's care and that we are being heard whether relief happens immediately or over time.

When we surrender to what is, we immerse ourselves in our entire being without compromise. We no longer pick and choose pieces that we prefer, to suit our tastes. Surrender does not have to come from suffering. When we resist anything is when we create the deep suffering within us.

Many think it is easier to jump on the train that is moving at full speed. But for those who get on board when the train is moving slowly, even going uphill, the gifts will be more magnificent. Riding a train moving slowly and purposefully, even one that seems to stall, will need our patience and endurance until the engine once again is filled with life's energy and fuel. When we jump on at full speed, we seem to be moving quicker, and this excites the ego, for the ego does not like to wait. But always, the train will slow down, and the ego will get off in the same place it started, impatient and rebuffed. Like the ebb and flow of life, when the train slows at our stop, is it not easier to come aboard?

Yet the truth is, we are never standing still. Like the piece of furniture that appears to be solid, deep within there are atoms moving at rapid speed. So fret not that life has brought everything to a perceived standstill.

What shall you do while it all appears stationary? This is a chance for you to meet me, take me into your body and soul and receive all the grace that I carry. For it is here that I pass it on to you with love and compassion. It is not for me to hold on to but to share with you. It is here that you know I have been here all along, waiting for you to come aboard.

We often move at a snail's pace to give you time to release all that is not yours, to throw any luggage off the train that you do not need. Know that through me and with me, to-gether, we will begin to pick up speed on the journey up the hill of our ascension. While there is no end point, we will be picking up speed. Know that you will move quickly at that time when you can allow all to unfold perfectly. You will be thankful for the moments you had with me when it was quiet, when the train was moving slowly, if not seemingly standing still.

Trust that that which goes up must come down; that which slows down eventually picks up speed. Trust that I will not let go of your hand. Trust that the slower we go, the more time we have to prepare for what is to unfold. Trust that we are never stationary when we are connecting with our heart and soul.

When our mind gives us a question, it is for our heart to answer. You have tamed the lion within your soul, now welcome it into your heart as you would the lamb. We look to others at times to blame for our misery, but they are simply a mirror for us to see what we need to become, to heal, to know within ourselves. When we feel anger towards another, we need only ask, where do we feel this anger within ourselves? This holds true for all our emotions.

When we feel love and compassion for others, we first feel it the most within ourselves. There is no bad or good out there, for in God's eyes, all is welcome. All is pure. All is whole. What we have asked others to do, they will oblige, and this is the greatest gift we can receive.

Through your trust and belief in God, peace will find its way into your heart and answers to your life issues will make themselves known to you in the form of an idea, a helping hand, or a different path than your current one. And in surrendering to God's will, you will feel joy and love as never before. Your heart will soar, your eyes will smile, and no matter what life brings your way, you will be happy. Yes, this is not only possible, but it is also your birthright.

Bless you, my child. Rest upon your knees until you no longer need to humble yourself into surrender. And then rest some more until you see a hand in front of you. Then you may take it and walk hand in hand with God, who always keeps you safe within His heart.

Christ Consciousness

REFLECTION

Alicia shared with Beth how profoundly this Sacred Letter had affected her when she read it. She felt compassion, an opening to higher possibilities, and began to see God and Love as interchangeable. It renewed her faith and her belief that she was always cared for, even in the darkest hours, awakening a new sense of hope. She shared that she was beginning to feel self-love and worthiness again. It reaffirmed the power of trusting in an all-loving God, knowing that regardless of what transpired, she was not alone, and was being guided with love.

STEVEN

TRUSTING OUR HEART

*"The space where we meet each other in love,
the deepest love imaginable. The space where we would
do the unthinkable for each other. Tear our hearts open
so we can meet together in a space like no other."*

—Steven

Beth and I joined a small class to work with a gifted medium to expand our abilities to communicate with the spiritual realm. During a group meditation, we were prompted to ask, "Who is my spirit guide?" I admit that, for me, it took months to discover the identity of my spirit guide. We all have one. But connecting to spirits without overthinking and analyzing takes patience and practice.

Interestingly, the others in the group felt confident that the names of the guides they were receiving were notable American Indians. Beth, however, kept hearing, "Smelly Bigfoot." She could feel the energy of a child, playful and utterly pleased with the idea that as hard as Beth tried to connect, he would slip into her thoughts with the funny name. Beth said she could hear a child laughing, as if delighted by the silliness.

Soon afterward, it became clear that the spirit was Steven, a young boy who had passed from cancer at the age of nine. He was the son of Ellen, one of our friends in the group. The boy's energy continued to linger in Beth's awareness after the workshop.

Beth would later remark to me how Steven's words seemed wise, far beyond his earthly years. The soul of a child can convey such profound wisdom that it seems to defy logic. Spirits of children ask us to feel their words and the magnificence of their soul through our hearts, not our minds. They encourage us to have faith, knowing that God will always sustain us, especially when the seemingly unimaginable happens—like the passing of a child.

Steven's Letter (May 2017)

Dear Mom,

This is what I would like to tell you. We are not our bodies and what we both experienced while I was in my body on earth was painful beyond words. Why did we have to go through that? Why me? Why you? I hear you asking these questions. And you need to know that it was me that had to go through it. The lesson was for me. You agreed to be there with me—one of the most selfless things a mom can do for a child.

When we heal and move beyond the experience, often the heartache is there. Perhaps it will always be there. Through the eyes of my sister and brothers, through the trips and gatherings, through the day in day out moments of life, I will always be there, calling you to come to me. But it does not have to be heartache. It does not have to be longing. It can be just the simple space that you and I share—always. The space where we meet each other in love, the deepest love imaginable. The space where we would do the unthinkable for each other. Tear our hearts open so we can meet together in a space like no other. So when you think of me, in sorrow or in joy, go to that space. It means I am calling you, or your soul is calling me. This is the sign. The thought of me, a memory, a song, a feeling—meet me in that space. Sit and meditate and open up to where that space is. You will be shown and it will be known. And then it will become more familiar, easier for you to find me.

As my body breaks down all that I am not, my soul fills up with all that I am. There is something about the snow that fills my soul. I know you love the beach and warmth, but I continue to cherish the time in the snow. There is something so pure and white, and like nothing I had experienced before this life. It was different.

Mom, I take your hand and we walk down the path together. I bring you to what looks like a bulls-eye target, the kind that is shot with arrows. I hand you the bow and arrow and watch you shoot, missing the target. You grow tired. Your fingers hurt. It gets dark. But you shoot, arrow after arrow, not wanting to give up. It rains. It snows. Spring comes and summer. You do not sway from your stance, trying to hit the target. I come to you and move your bow just a few inches up. You pull back and shoot. Bull's eye.

There are children everywhere. Some of them dying early in their lives, some of them living for a long time. It appears that there is no rhyme or reason for it. We are all God's children weaving our way through the tapestry of time. There is no way to understand through reason. We must put our faith in God's hands and know that we are all his children, and there is always a purpose beyond our understanding. So we must continue on with our hearts open, knowing and having faith that there is a higher order. We must leave our minds to tend to everyday tasks, while our hearts grab ahold of something bigger and spin us around until we don't know which end is up or down—until the confusion comes, and out of this confusion comes clarity. And out of clarity comes the only thing that matters—the space where we, you and I, meet in love and laughter.

There is always baseball. This sticks in my mind. Along with cotton candy, rough housing, summer, popsicles, and snuggling beneath a blanket as the snow falls outside. I am with you always. Now and always. Never to be forgotten, never to be far from view.

The last thing I leave you with is patience. All will come in the moment it is meant and at the perfect time. The hours we fill up to avoid the void is where impatience shows itself. When we rest in the moments, the hours are full. I see you by a tree Mom, nurturing and being nurtured. You are so beautiful. You are so full of light. Patience will allow us to move from one moment to the next when we are guided, not when we rush.

Don't I talk old now, Mom? Don't mistake my words that Beth has put into writing as not sounding like me. For like you, I have my soul, my all-knowing part of me, and my fun childlike part of me. Both are available. Just like it is for you and everyone else who is alive on earth. Too many live from one or the other. But a balance is important. Like going on a teeter-totter at the playground. When it is in balance, and everyone is working together, it goes smoothly. Sometimes we are up and other times down. We each get our turn. And like the teeter-totter, we need to know that this too will pass. When we feel down, we will go back up. One is not better or worse. Both are necessary to play the game and have fun. And it is the patience I spoke about before that allows us to go through the darkness, the not so fun spots, knowing that we will always be up again.

Release the "should have been" and allow the divine to guide you in every moment. Pray for strength but know that you have always been courageous. Even when it seems that all the cards are stacked against you, know you are given nothing that you cannot handle. Divinity is within and without, always guiding, nurturing, and holding you in love. And I am right here. I am by your side. In fact, I never left.

You are never alone and always loved.

Trust that all is well, that love rises to the top.

Steven

REFLECTION

Steven, with his mischievous sense of humor and childlike joy, often came into Beth's awareness long after his letter was transcribed. Sometimes bringing forth more messages for his mother; other times, just reminding Beth that he is here—whole, pure, and happy. Beth relayed messages to Ellen about how he often joined his family around the breakfast table, eating pancakes, his favorite. Or that he would be joining her at a soccer game she was to attend for his sister. Beth could envision him sitting on his mom's lap, enjoying her company.

Ellen had been asking for a sign to let her know that Steven was alive and well. Amazingly, the very next morning, Steven came through with a message for his mother. As Beth was listening to Ellen describe the unusual angel-shaped forms in the snow on the fence in her backyard, she sensed Steven stepping forward. He told Beth that he had created the shapes of angels on the wood. It was a message to his mother that he was present, a comforting reminder that our soul lives on, as does our joy and love for one another.

ARCHANGEL GABRIEL

BECOMING VULNERABLE

"Open yourself up to all that you are in each moment."

— Archangel Gabriel

All of us have many angels and spirits surrounding us, guiding us with unconditional love. They watch over and protect us according to what works best for our personality and purpose in life. Beth and I have heard from different people who were aware of their guardian angel. Some shared that they felt their angel was more "hands-on," while others have felt them to be more of an observer. It is never too late to invite them in. Call upon them with gratitude for their inspiration, protection, and guidance. You will always be met with their unconditional love, accepting you exactly as you are. For these angelic beings want nothing more than to serve and guide you to your perfect self.

Early on in our experience of connecting with the unseen realm, Beth received this message for me from Archangel Gabriel. Many believe that angels are neither male nor female but embody characteristics of both genders, though one gender may come through more strongly to the person in touch with an angel. Both Beth and I could feel Archangel Gabriel's feminine energy and love.

Beth was told many years ago, during a session with an intuitive healer, that Archangel Gabriel was one of her main guiding angels. When Beth learned to practice Shamanic journeying, over the course of months, she sensed the presence of this angel. Beth could see Gabriel's red flowing hair and beautiful layered garments as this archangel led her to the building that held the Akashic Records, the great book documenting our present, past, and future lives. In this Sacred Letter, Beth was receiving information from my own Akashic Record.

During the final phase of completing our book, Archangel Gabriel appeared to Beth in a meditation. At that moment, Beth felt Gabriel's excitement that she had so beautifully received everything the angel had shown her. Confirming, too, that she was indeed the author of this Sacred Letter.

Archangel Gabriel's Letter
(November 2016)

Dear Berit,

We smile as we write this and hope that this comes through in our letter. Your heart is made of gold. Your eyes brighten those you see. Your smile triggers light within each soul you encounter.

To know the frown as the smile, the tears as the laughter, and hate as love is to be human. To know all is divine and to allow the feelings to come and go like the wind. We told you that all is there upon the carpet; for at times you do go looking further than need be. But also know that sometimes we need to lift the carpet to look for what we might have swept underneath it.

Often something of discomfort is swept away, to be dealt with at a later time. These do not go away but gather dust and grow bigger. They remain there until we lift the carpet and ask, what is there for me to clear and clean? What do I need to do?

Sit before the dust gathered in front of you. Touch it, feel it. Rub it between your fingers. Do not shy away or run for the vacuum, but feel the dirt and grime. Feel how it feels upon your skin, within your truest knowing. We cannot know joy without anger, or courage without fear, or cooperation without competition. These seemingly opposite emotions are entwined together until we release all judgment. We need both, for we cannot know one without the other. Over time, when all emotions are accepted into your heart, you will no longer need to feel what seems to be negative.

Even a clown has tears; in fact, these are most often hidden behind the mask of laughter. When the tears emerge, especially from a clown, most people will not like it or want it, for it seems like it does not belong. This is what will occur at first, as you uncover what is beneath the carpet, but know that if others feel put off, then you are on the right track. You are uncovering a piece of you that helps you to become whole once more.

To repeat, every emotion is divine—both jealousy and admiration, anger and peace, hate and love. You will not have to go looking for this. Just open yourself up to all that you are in each moment and you will be given this chance to enlarge your heart to fit everything into your being.

You are such beauty—like morning birds singing in the sunlight. Go out into the world and do what you do, but do not forget to bring all of you. The melodies will be even more beautiful, the lyrics divinely guided, and those who listen will be gifted with the most beautiful messages imaginable.

We are so proud of you for following through in all you have received from us. You are opening up and following through in what is brought to you on so many levels. You radiate love and beauty, and this is felt not only by souls that you connect with every day, but it is truly felt around the globe. Each breath of love, each word of praise and gratefulness, each notion of connection to the higher realms allows your light to flow across the globe with grace and ease. It is felt by the child who hungers for a meal, as well as by the older man in need of a human voice to break the depth of his silence.

You hold the key to spreading light and love upon a planet that is awakening, and the key is within your heart. Your mission is as obvious as the smile you see upon another's face or the tear of appreciation falling down someone's cheek. You are on the right course and doing all we have hoped for you and more. Grab the hands of those around you that open them to you, but also do not be afraid to walk ahead, and guide. You are a way shower. You are doing great things. Keep to the path, and your heart will lead the way.

We hold you in our dearest softest embraces each and every moment. You are held. You are loved. You are cherished. You are doing all we could ask for.

Bless you, my beautiful child. We honor you. You are worth your weight in gold.

What will unfold for you, you cannot imagine. But try, for all we see and know is all we are capable of achieving.

Love to you our beloved.

Archangel Gabriel

REFLECTION

Following this Sacred Letter, Beth continued to feel Archangel Gabriel more than ever. Not long after, in a meditation, Beth was led to a mountain and up a winding road that took her to the top of a high cliff. She wasn't aware why she was there, but she remembers looking out across the view and into the deep abyss below.

Then, all of a sudden, she knew that she was supposed to jump. So she did! Beth had confided in me that she felt guided to go deeper into her faith in this lifetime. Falling down into this deep chasm, she was caught by Archangel Gabriel. She scooped up Beth in her wing and placed her upon a cloud where Archangel Michael stood. He told Beth that to live fearlessly is to have a leap of faith!

I, too, continue to feel Archangel Gabriel's splendid energy; like sparkling light radiating within my aura around the right side of my head and shoulder. She guides me with feelings, words, and images, encouraging me to expand beyond my own thinking and limitations, which helps me open further to receive and deliver messages.

Archangel Gabriel was the catalyst for a most unusual spiritual experience that occurred weeks later. While out walking in my neighborhood, I felt as if my physical body had expanded to the size of New Jersey! I could turn my head to the left and see the southern Jersey shoreline; to the right, the Delaware Water Gap. It was mind-bending. I had never experienced anything like that before, nor have I since. I later realized that it was to give me the experience of not being limited in physical form or thought. To embody great expanse!

I am forever grateful to Archangel Gabriel, as I know that she is helping direct the messages I receive. She is a gate-keeper in my interactions with those here in my earthly life as well as with those in the heavens. She opens my awareness to so much that lies within the unseen and guides my movements up and down my Jacob's ladder, an image that Beth had been given for me from Archangel Gabriel. Archangel Gabriel continues to tell me that there are many leading me to where and when I am to deliver messages.

PETER

HEALING FROM ADDICTIONS

"There is nothing to fix, there is everything to feel."

— Peter

My cousin Peter passed into the afterlife without a goodbye. A drug overdose on January 27, 2017, abruptly ended his promising young life. Over time, the powerful prescription pain medication given to Peter after a car accident created a dangerous chemical and emotional bondage that seemed unbreakable. Despite his efforts, he could not shake the addiction, and he slipped from the world, leaving behind unimaginable grief for all those that knew this sweet young man so full of potential.

Everyone loved Peter. He was a quiet, wonderfully kind, unpretentious guy. Sixteen years my junior, Peter loved his family and friends. He had a big heart and thought the best of everyone, without judgment. Peter was a gifted athlete and an avid fisherman, and he was especially devoted to his dogs.

Days before Peter's passing, he had asked his parents whether he could attend church with them that coming Sunday. They were overjoyed, of course. He would indeed return to his family's church, but sadly, for his own memorial service.

The eulogy at Peter's service challenged us not to judge, but love; to be that friend and beacon of hope, while never giving up on anyone. The following words, written by Peter's parents, call for self-reflection and unconditional love.

We ask, is life for each of us like living in a forest, a forest made up of our God given genes, strengths, weaknesses, values, hopes, and chosen community?

We ask, how honest are we with ourselves in describing the forest we live in?

We ask, how willing are we to seek a forest of life more suited to who we really are and want to be?

We ask, how well do we know the forests that others live in?

We ask, whom else do we ask to help us to at least talk about these questions?

We ask, can we be honest with others and ourselves?

We ask, where in this forest where we live are there beacons of light and hope?

We ask, do we allow ourselves to look for the beacons, to see them, to follow them?

Friends, if you know of someone like our Peter, love them. Don't judge them. Do what you can for them. Sacrifice for them, do things with them, be their friend, be a beacon in their forest. Never give up on them. Never!

It's often hard, but every ounce you put into it is worth it.

We ask that Peter be remembered for who he was and all those wonderful qualities. Not for the circumstances of how he died. Dear God, we ask. May it be so. Amen.

After his passing, Peter channeled three Sacred Letters to Beth, including these insightful words: "The drug epidemic is widespread and far more malignant than anything else going on in the world, and leading all into the world of falsehood, the sense that is not real or true about life. But it is for innocent reasons—to feel the unconditional love, unity, and aliveness that nobody feels. To be home again."

Peter's Letter (February 2017)

Dear Brothers and Sisters:

Can you feel the pain? The heartache deep within? It is there. Just buried beneath the layers of neglected emotion. For each time we push aside the pain, sadness, or anger, it burrows like a termite, creating holes within us. And we try to fill up these holes with stuff—admiration, food, drugs, work, technology. But this is only a temporary fix. We can see these holes in most everyone who walks the planet and it takes time and effort to uncover these holes.

It seems like many energy workers who walk the planet try to unstick some sort of stuck energy. I want you to know this leads to a false sense of what is really going on. For the energy is not stuck, it has just created a hole. So when someone comes for help with an addiction, the first thing we must do is get him to stop trying to fill the hole with outside stuff. We cannot help until this is done. Once we encourage them to stop filling the hole, we can help them find their way back to being "whole."

We do this by two methods—self-reflection and feeling. Self-reflection is not necessary in the sense of going back and rehashing all the drama or actions, but to become aware of their feelings. Once a feeling arises, to feel that feeling. So often this feeling we feel in the present is simply one from the past. For whatever we have not resolved from the past, we bring into our lives to heal.

For instance, if we had an alcoholic father or a mother with a personality disorder, we may find ourselves dating someone or becoming friends with someone with these traits. This is to allow ourselves the path to healing; but we must be able to make this connection, or the past repeats itself. We succumb to the conditioning that we have always known, without moving forward in our healing. This place of "stuckness" is where we create drama. We become addicted, we act out, we react, hurt others, we hurt ourselves; we try and fill our hole with anything and everything, anyone and everyone. It is within this hole that we feel like we are not enough.

And when we try and fill our hole, over and over, we end up with a false sense of who we are. We wear a mask every day. We pretend we are not powerful. We feel separated and disconnected from our self and our souls. We wind up confused, alone. We walk around shaming others, as we have been shamed. We hurt others, as we have been hurt. We have relationships that are shallow and meaningless, plagued with drama. We try and control others. We don't honor them for who they are, for we do not honor ourselves. Until we have had enough. Until we know that we are enough.

The bigger the hole, the stronger the wall around our heart. For what we don't realize until we become aware of our emotions is that we are already whole. We are just one tear away from being reunited, reconnected with our hearts and true selves. There is nothing to fix, there is everything to feel. It is that simple.

We have just forgotten how to feel. How to let our true self shine through. How to open our heart no matter who is ready to stomp on it because they are in pain and afraid to feel themselves. We have forgotten the beauty in tears, the magnificent release of pain, which leads us down the path to wholeness. We have forgotten our connection with our higher selves, our souls, our divinity. We have forgotten because we have separated ourselves, split ourselves off from our emotion, which disconnects us as humans from ourselves and each other.

And each time we reach for that slot machine, that needle, that piece of cake, that smart phone, we reinforce that we need to fill ourselves up with stuff to feel enough. But we wind up further and further down deep within our own hole, having no idea who we are or how unbelievably amazing and powerful and loved we are.

Yes, it is simple, not easy but simple. I am encouraging you to feel. Just feel. Move from your head to your heart.

Put down your pain so you can see it, touch it, taste it, and allow it once again become part of you. For deep within this pain is the most incredible joy you have ever felt. It is where love, connection, true beauty, inspiration, creativity, light, and happiness live.

It is through our feelings, including the pain, that we come to know that we are enough.

You are not alone.

You are so loved.

I lend you the courage to find your heart and allow it all back in, until you can find your own. You just have to surrender and say, I have had enough!

This is the path to freedom. This is the path to joy. This is the path to wholeness.

Peter

REFLECTION

We all know someone who is dealing with addiction or has been affected by addiction. We are witnessing an unprecedented drug epidemic that is sweeping across America like wildfire, destroying beautiful lives and leaving all of those in its wake dazed, exhausted, heart-broken, or dead. Those who have lost their way are the ones that we must bring back into our community. We are all necessary and bound together in an extraordinary, sacred connection. We must not abandon anyone, but instead, help each person reclaim their glory, holding them in the highest light until they find their way back to their true self.

GRANDMA RUTH

LIVING FEARLESSLY

"Stop playing with fear. You don't need it.
It is not real. It is not you."

— Grandma Ruth

Seven years after her Grandma Ruth's passing, Beth felt her presence for the first time. While making oatmeal, Grandma Ruth's specialty, Beth heard a soft, gentle instruction to use water along with the milk. Moments before, Beth had been wondering why each time she prepared oatmeal it was burning the bottom of the pan. Beth laughed. She knew immediately it was Grandma Ruth.

Their relationship was special, close. Growing up, Beth travelled to Florida to be with her grandmother during family vacations, enjoying swimming, tram rides, and playing shuffleboard and card games. Later on, while attending graduate school in Florida, Beth often visited Grandma Ruth.

Upon her death, Beth received a collection of her grandmother's writings, including thoughts about fear that she had written when she was twenty-two years old as part of a class assignment. The following is dated April 15, 1930:

"The adult laughs at those childish fears which he has now outgrown cower before the ones confronting him. Life seems to be a series of battles with fears from which we usually emerge battered and broken."

Now, from the other side, Beth felt her grandmother's spirit. Wiser, and coming from a different perspective, she encourages all of us to release fear and false beliefs. Grandma Ruth shared the truth that fear does not have to break us, for it is but an illusion.

GRANDMA RUTH'S LETTER (DECEMBER 2016)

Dear Little Ones,

Here I am. I am still here. But I worried all of my life about dying and death. I did enjoy life at times, in spite of myself (Beth heard her laughing). Many times. But there was this piece of me that was always pinned to the earth in fear.

Do not live your life in fear. I had lived my life in fear and none of it came true. It prevented me from truly being present, being there as myself. Our mind has a mind of its own. It is like an animal that needs to be tamed. No, not tamed, but trained.

Stop playing with fear. You don't need it. It is not real. It is not you. You are love. You are light. You are laughter. If you let fear be, then it will leave you be. If you stop running from fear, it will stop chasing you. It is simple actually. Worry and stay in fear, and you will feel fear; you will close yourself off from all possibilities for living a life full of love and laughter. Leave fear to fend for itself and it will grow bored, tired of your lack of attention. It will go off to find someone better to play with.

We need to let ourselves fly to see what we are capable of, to truly know ourselves in the eyes of our soul. Even if we fall, it is better than not trying. Life will bring you much to conquer. This is the truth. But can you move and continue in the face of fear, even if it shakes your foundation like an earthquake? Can you step aside the rubble and see what needs to be rebuilt? What can be saved and what needs to be tossed aside? There is nothing more disruptive than an earthquake, shaking up the ground, forcing those to start from a new world, a different place. Shaking up the foundation—that is what is going on in the world today.

It is like pulling the carpet out from under our feet, shaking up fear, hatred, and evil. We can land on our backs, but then, that is exactly where we need to be. It is the closest way to get us to our knees, where we surrender to all we are and will be and ask for strength to face our fears head on.

So go out and live fearlessly. You are not alone.

Grandma Ruth

REFLECTION

Beth and I both felt gratitude for the simple truth of Grandma Ruth's candid message: become fearless. Such a simple message but perhaps the most challenging!

Identifying in fear pulls us down and drains our power, handicapping us from expressing the fullness of who we each are, with all of our creative gifts and visions. This important message coming from spirit reminds us that it is never too late to recognize and then release the chains of fear that bind us.

PART THREE

CONNECTING WITH
ALL THERE IS

"We must have faith and follow our soul, that voice,
that intuition, that gentle urging that encourages us to look
and go beyond what we see and know."

—Louise

SOMMER

(THE DOG)

SHARING OUR SPACE

"Whether we are human or animal is not important.
We are all created as spiritual beings."

— Sommer (the Dog)

The messages that Beth and I receive are as remarkable as the spirits who communicate them. On occasion, we receive a message from a person who is still alive, or even from an animal. While walking our dogs one autumn afternoon, Beth was surprised to connect with Sommer, my golden retriever, who had been undergoing chemotherapy after being diagnosed with cancer. The telepathic communication from this living creature was strong and immediate, urging Beth to take note of all that my dog was sharing as we walked together in the woods that day.

Not only was Sommer aware that we had been receiving the Sacred Letters, but she also was one step ahead of us; she communicated to Beth that she too would dictate a letter. A few days later, Sommer channeled this Sacred Letter to give to my daughter Sarah. Sommer passed the following January.

Sommer's Letter (October 2017)

Dear Sarah,

We are all the same. Unique in our mission, but the same within our hearts. We are all children of God and were created to learn, grow, and evolve. Whether we are human or animal is not important. We are all created as spiritual beings. We cannot strive to become like God because we already are God. We are meant to live in harmony with each other as fellow humans and animals. We are meant to share our space—to learn, love, and teach each other.

As a human being, you can turn a blind eye or hide your head in the sand when you do not want to feel. We are here, as animals, to show what it means to love unconditionally. Opening our hearts is not a choice for us. We don't choose to show our love or not. We just are love. We live in packs and need each other as much as you need each other. We are here to help you all remove your heads from the sand and open your hearts. To reach out to each other within your communities so that you can see you are not alone.

We share our space and hearts with you as much as you share your homes with us. We dogs and cats have come here to live in harmony with humans, but we have also come here in service to all. We connect and are living as we are guided. At times, we are strays and we find companions, and at other times, we are born into loving homes, cared for, and treated with the highest form of veterinary care, and then given away to loving homes. Our beginnings do not matter to us, as we always end up exactly where we are supposed to be for the connection we make with those humans who we share our lives with.

I have chosen to live with you and our loving dear family. It was not long ago that you received a cancer diagnosis. I agreed to help you heal by helping to take this cancer from you both physically and emotionally. This could not have made me happier, as this was my service for you. Like you, I experienced the highest of care with chemotherapy treatment and chose this in order to experience this type of healing for my own spiritual growth.

What I would like to share is that knowing I received this cancer diagnosis is not bad. Most would say it is not good, but I am here to tell you that I am joyful whether I have a diagnosis or not. I do not think about what it all means, for I know this is just in my path and it is teaching me some very important lessons about what it felt like for you to go through cancer and treatment. I wanted to feel this directly, as I wanted to help you heal, as it was my job.

One only has to look at a dog or cat, a family pet, to see that it has taken on either a physical or emotional issue from its owners. This is what transpires so often when we share our space. This is why dogs and cats have moved into their homes, to become closer and experience our lessons as well as helping you in a more direct capacity, as we used to be more wild. Our roles as pets have changed.

We have become teachers, guides, and healers for our families as well as whatever we are to learn for our own spiritual lessons. It can be as simple as showing what it means to have unconditional love and friendship or as complicated as taking on a cancer diagnosis.

How I feel while going to chemotherapy treatment is that I take in everything while I am receiving treatment. For the treatment is far more than the medicine I receive. It is the caring nature of those administering the treatment, as well as those around me. It is those I meet while there as well as those I pass by.

We also cannot forgo what a powerful healer love and

compassion can be, as well as prayer and social support. Love puts us within the highest vibration, and this is where the greatest healing occurs, where the intelligence of the body takes over and helps to heal what is out of balance.

Can you put aside anxieties and fears and drink in the love and compassion from those who sit to your left and right? Can you know there is a higher purpose for being where you are and ask what that may be? Can you see their bodies full of health and abundance and bless them with wholeness? Can you do this with everyone you meet?

All of this will open the door for learning how to bless and love yourself.

We are all light, love, and children of God.

Yes, we share the space in our homes with our families. We get sick, too. Sometimes we get better and heal and sometimes we move on. It is not the outcome but the lessons we learn along with way that remain the most important thing about life on earth.

I am so grateful for you, our family, the service I have provided and the space that we have shared both in our home and in our hearts.

When people look into each other's eyes, they can see through to the soul. The love is in there. And that remains whether they are sick or healthy. Whether they have cancer or allergies. Whether they are big or small. Wild or tame. We, as dogs and cats, have come to shower everyone with love and help all to love themselves and each other. For without love, there can be no healing.

Be gentle in your ways and loving with yourself.

When we can love ourselves beyond all else, win over our own hearts, it is then we can go forth and share our love.

Our world is so beautiful, yet out of balance. This is true for many of us, even down to our bodies. Once we become more balanced and connected to the whole, the wrongs become right, the sickness becomes health, the war becomes peace, and the complacency becomes action. And the love rises above everything else.

We are all masters. We are all creators. We are all one.

I love you Sarah.

Sommer

REFLECTION

Beth and I were surprised by the content in this message. Admittedly, the words did not sound as if they were coming from a dog. Sommer challenged our beliefs about animals as spiritual beings. All the same, we promised to deliver the message to Sarah that came through from her.

The following January, on the morning before Sommer

was laid to rest, Beth and her intuitive son Drew came to say goodbye. Sommer gave them clear messages about lions. Saying goodbye to our pets is never easy, but both Beth and I felt Sommer was letting us know she was ready to run again, to be free from pain and illness.

I shared with my husband the message about the lion that Beth and her son had received the morning of Sommer's passing, as well as a photo Beth had taken of Sommer's footprints on our snowy front walk. While my husband was driving home that evening, a song came on the radio that he had never heard before and it caught his attention. It was singer-songwriter Bruce Cockburn's 1979 hit, "Wondering Where the Lions Are." My husband's tears fell.

Later, when looking up the album online, he found another timely song, "No Footprints." Sharing the lyrics with me, he confided in astonishment that perhaps, for the first time, he was receiving clear messages from the spiritual realm—from Sommer. Wherever he turned after Sommer's passing, he felt her strong presence in everything, from songs on the radio to TV commercials showing golden retrievers. They caught his attention and he remarked with a laugh that Sommer was "dogging" him. He could not deny the comfort he felt from this communication. Cockburn's songs had validated my husband's own intuitive power to hear and feel our beloved Sommer.

We all continue to feel Sommer, her spirit now free and light.

SYDNEY

WALKING WITH MOTHER EARTH

"What we do to the earth, we do to ourselves."

— Sydney

While out walking one day, I noticed two hawks circling overhead. I am always in awe of the impressive silhouette of their expansive wings against the sky. It reminded me of the image of a magnificent hawk that I had been given after my niece asked me to connect with her deceased friend, a student named Sydney, who had died in the 2015 earthquake in Nepal. Sydney and a friend had taken a gap year before starting college and were trekking through the Langtang Valley in Nepal when a magnitude 7.8 earthquake struck, killing more than 8,000 people, including these two Americans.

When Sydney came into my awareness, there was a freshness, simplicity, and joy about her. I felt her sense of conviction and optimism and was struck by a profound feeling of what it means to cherish another person. I heard the name "Paul," and would later learn that he was one of her two cherished brothers. Sydney's energy sparkled with excitement, as if eagerly waiting to communicate what she was feeling.

I described to Beth the images and sensations I had received about Sydney and her friend. I saw the girls clasp hands and felt their deep gratitude for one another, as if forever bonded in their friendship and love. I felt the gravity of the grief left in the wake of their passing as well as the outpouring of love from people across the globe. Though not fully understanding all of it, I sensed the magnitude of what Sydney and her friend had done in their young lives and how powerfully these two girls had impacted others' lives.

It was clear that Sydney's spirit had a strong connection with the earth. Later, during a meditation, Beth was taken to the middle of a deep forest where she could see mountain peaks. Images of the greenest of trees and bluest of oceans came into her awareness. As she waded in warm water, she was met by Sydney, who had brought Beth into this scene to feel the nourishing spirit of nature by using all of her senses.

The words of this Sacred Letter from Sydney flowed

through later that day. Thoughtful and confident, Sydney was cheering us on, not only to honor ourselves but also to celebrate the beauty of our earth.

Sydney's Letter (August 2017)

Dear Human Race:

I am here! You cannot see me, but I am still here. I lived my life with passion and love. One cannot know their fate or when they may leave this earth. It is not predictable, nor should it be. There is always a piece of us that knows but keeps it hidden from our mind. We have to. Our lives would not be genuine if we knew when we would leave this planet; it would be like reading the last chapter of a book first.

The accomplishment is in the journey, not the outcome. It is in the not knowing but doing it anyway. It is saying yes to fear and having it not stop you. There are some that will let fear stop them in living their lives to the fullest. I simply ask you the question, For what purpose? To live a life that is safe, not taking risks, not moving outside the box that keeps us small and insecure. Yes, not secure but insecure. We think it will enable us to stay here on earth, but what kind of life is that? One that keeps our heart closed and our minds locked inside the box of unknowing.

Living a life that is safe, not taking risks, not discovering all we are about—our earth, our families, our lives—keeps us small and insecure. We need to live a passionate life, experiencing the wonder of it all. Discovering, learning, falling down, and getting back up again.

Enjoy what this earth has to offer—amazing food, beautiful rivers, and incredible sunsets. Explore our beautiful land. Wade through the heavenly waters. Listen to the redwoods standing tall and proud in our mighty forests. Ascend to the top of our snow-capped mountains and raise your arms in gratitude for all of creation. Upon your descent, allow the sun to guide you to pathways and journeys you have yet to explore. Open up to all the beauty and magnificence. Intertwine your bodies with the earth, releasing anything unnecessary into the fires of your soul. Connect your soul with the heart of our heavens and earth, cherishing all within your very being.

Turn towards our land and not against each other. Fight for its beauty and preserve its history. Listen to it breathe. Our lands, our waters, our mountains are living, breathing, beings. We suffocate with our ignorance, destroying all that our earth has given to us. We take without replacing and kill without thought.

Our animals, beings of light and love, get it. We must get it before it is too late. We must dare to open our hearts to the beauty of a bird's song, take in the colors of flowers, and stand in solidarity with our animals. We must listen to their cries for help and answer the call of the wild.

Mother Earth is not angry, she does not force her emotions by way of earthquakes or tornadoes, tsunamis, or heat waves. She only forces what she can in the wake of destruction. To be destroyed is to die and then to begin again. These storms are a clearing of all that was that was not of the highest vibration. It is a warning, a message to get on board or be swept away from all we know.

I have come back to relay this message, for my voice can be heard. I speak for Mother Earth, as we often do not listen to her cries. We must open our eyes to the ignorance that has come before us and collectively put forth our efforts to heal our planet, as we heal ourselves. For what we do to the earth, we do to ourselves. We cannot honor ourselves while we hurt those beings and life around us. We project our pain unto our world, without meaning. We must remember why we are here and awaken to our bigger purpose.

Healing comes not from keeping our hearts closed and our eyes skewed, but from awakening and opening ourselves up to life. It comes from saying no to fear and limits; it happens by becoming one with our beautiful earth and respecting all species. Nothing and nobody are ever in our way but are there to remind us.

There are no enemies. The fighting must stop. When we pick up a sword, we make an enemy out of each other—disrespecting and disagreeing, needing to be right. But what if what was right was to just be, and honor and pray and bless and appreciate all in our lives?

What if our earth continues to crumble beneath our feet and erupt in the most obvious way possible so that change must come? And it must come now. Is it not obvious? The melting of the ice caps, the damaging of our air, and polluting of our water. The earth has spoken. She has warned. She is fighting for her life—but do not blame her. The massive storms, climate change causing death and destruction, is all she is left with to get our attention. It is a warning that must be heeded. Human consumption is but a selfish notion to take without giving; competition separates our hearts into the haves and have nots.

We are all One and when we hurt another, we hurt ourselves. Feel the winds of those that have come before and learn from them. Release what no longer serves. Make a decision to change and do it. Now. It is never too late. Anything is possible. We just need to put down our weapons of ignorance and selfishness and pick up the pieces of our hearts.

Start today. Start small. Forgive. Love. Honor. Respect.

Will you live a life of suffering and inflict hurt upon the earth? Or will you open your hearts and respect the miracles of life in all that has been given? It is ours to cherish till death do us part. A bond forever graced, in love and awe.

Sydney

DAWN

HONORING THE BODY

"Our bodies are here with us on our journey as our guides,
leading and helping us to learn about ourselves
and discover what we came here to do."

— Dawn

It was the woman's long blond braid that would unravel the mystery behind the spirit who kept appearing to Beth when we were connecting to Sydney, the college student in the previous letter who had passed in the 2015 earthquake in Nepal. Beth would ask, "Who is the woman with the blonde hair braid?"

When Beth brought her into my awareness, I could see this woman on the left side of my visual field, but her personality felt older and different than the younger spirit I was speaking with.

Yet every time we would engage with Sydney, the woman with the long blond braid reappeared.

Weeks passed, and I still felt her presence, sensing a quiet strength and connection to the earth. Whenever I felt her energy, the song lyrics, "This is the dawning of the Age of Aquarius" played in my head, followed by images of Maine. I started to research Maine news. Had a woman from Maine also perished in that earthquake?

Upon searching the Internet, I found that a woman from Maine had indeed been lost in the earthquake. But what startled me was the photo above the article. There, standing on a cold summit in Nepal and gazing at the beautiful expanse of jagged mountain peaks, was the silhouette of a woman with a long blond braid! And her name was Dawn! No wonder I kept hearing the song lyrics about the "dawning" of the Aquarian age. The article explained that she had been hiking on the trail where the earthquake struck and that another hiker had taken this photograph on the summit days before.

I reached out to make contact with Dawn's adult children. I also wanted to share their mother's message to see if it resonated. Without any luck, I was just about to give up when I felt Dawn's presence and heard a clear, persistent word from her: "travel." Questions arose. I was then guided to do an Internet search that would connect her son with travel, and to my amazement, I found his travel company. Dawn had provided me with that missing link. In a phone conversation with her son, I shared the information I had received about Dawn's personality and later emailed him her Sacred Letter.

Dawn continues to return to Beth and me from time to time. Her presence is consistently loving and strong, bringing to mind the phrase "small, but mighty." She has woven an abundance of love into our body and soul, like the braiding of her long blond hair.

Dawn's Letter (September 2017)

Dear Beautiful Souls,

Our bodies are sacred. The ultimate goal for our souls to learn and grow is to care for our bodies, whether we inhabit our bodies for a lifetime or a moment. To come to earth and experience what we can, what we set out to do is a feat in itself. We are always at the right place at the right time when we enter and leave our bodies.

How we leave our bodies is planned by us well in advance. There is nothing haphazard; everything has a rhyme and reason. When we depart alone, we affect those around us dramatically with the grief we leave behind by our absence. For those that pass alone, this can feel very sacred, ceremonial, intimate. The method to how we leave our bodies is important. Do we go suddenly in an accident or perhaps experience a longer illness?

Some of us depart in pairs. This is often to aid those who have been left behind to lean on each other in their time of grief and mourning. Friends, coworkers, or even strangers can leave this planet two by two. This also enables the pair to travel together to the other side. While this is not always necessary, and there is no judgment as to how one leaves their body, it can provide comfort to those who cross over as well as those who still remain in their bodies.

To those that leave in groups—those that are victims of mass shootings or natural disasters, this has an immediate effect on their loved ones, but it also has a greater impact on the planet as a whole. Just to reiterate: All types of passing are necessary and often have more than one purpose and growth for those left behind.

We all feel bruised and battered when one of us departs. It is often the toughest part of being human and living upon this earth. But it is what we came here to do, to experience, to grow, and become, and there is no greater teacher than death.

We cannot talk about leaving our bodies without speaking about living within our bodies. Too often in our world today, our bodies have taken the brunt of our neglect and ignorance. We run too far, drink to excess, eat until we are uncomfortable, stuff all of our emotions down, blindly and coldly, and our bodies end up taking the brunt of it all. We are conditioned to live within the material world where so much is available for us to imbibe. It is not unusual for us to run into some trouble, a roadblock within our physical bodies, to wake us up and call us to look at how we are treating our bodies, and then to look beyond the physical.

Our bodies are doing so much more than we realize. This is why it is important to honor them and treat them with respect. Our bodies are here with us on our journey as our guides, leading and helping us to learn about ourselves, and discover what we came here to do. They are our surest soul companions that can provide us with messages and guidance on a daily basis. The more we engage in rituals, allowing our bodies to unite with the earth, the more connected we will feel to them.

We need to treat our bodies as we would our own children—with care, love, and nourishment. Too often, we separate ourselves as if our bodies are not extensions of ourselves. Yet, all that we experience can emotionally manifest itself within our bodies. The more we continue to neglect our true selves, and hide our vulnerability, the more aches and pains show up. Trauma, stranded emotions, and pain can transform, if not released, and become lodged within our bodies as blocks. This block will show up when it has reached its limit and we can find ourselves encountering an illness or disease.

We so often use our bodies for competition. We see who can be the thinnest, strongest, and prettiest, instead of celebrating our bodies for the beautiful, intelligent, and miraculous creations we inhabit. This vanity of the body keeps us small and unaware. When we open our minds and listen to our bodies, we can receive so many insights and messages. Our bodies can and will speak to us and let us know when they have had enough, when it is time to wake up. Do not become afraid or live in fear of our bodies taking on a disease, for when they begin to falter under the weight of dis-ease is the time to begin our journey back to ourselves. We then have the wonderful opportunity to work together with our bodies to bring our physical, emotional, and mental health back into unity.

Now is the time to celebrate our bodies, to love ourselves endlessly and fearlessly. But do so gently and lovingly. Do not run our bodies into the ground, but allow them to rise to the occasion, to move our energy and let our chi, our life force, flow. Move our bodies with grace and ease; allow them to teach us where we have fallen asleep. Care for our bodies with the highest love, compassion, and kindness, as we would a child or a small puppy.

It is good to receive medical help as well as energy work. Both are sacred. Both are often necessary. Be open to your body's guidance. When healing becomes necessary, whether one needs to rest in solitude, nourishment, or medical attention, listen to what is needed.

Release all shame and doubt associated with the body and align your soul with the magnitude of the body's intelligence that rests beyond our mind's awareness. Welcome miracles, while allowing for time to heal as well. Unravel yourself from the caverns of your mind's conditioning as blocks are released into the atmosphere.

Allow your body to take you to places, to meet people, and engage in all experiences to open up your mind. Allow your path to unfold, gather what you have learned, and all the while, continue to question what feels good to your body. What feels good in the body is what is good for the soul.

Whether it be to begin a gentle yoga practice or a walk in the woods—gentleness and ease is the new age of exercise.

We need to listen. Listen to what our bodies are saying. Listen with compassion.

Love and respect our bodies until that moment when it is time to leave our bodies behind, knowing they have served us beyond what they have been called to do. Their experiences have been ours as well and we could not have done it without them. Thank them, as their mission is the highest call from beyond—whether they carry us for a moment or a lifetime.

Lay your body upon our Mother Earth, drench it within her waters and soak up her love. Allow her to envelop your being, swallow you whole, as her awareness seeps into your own.

Life is sacred. Our tears are sacred. Our laughter is sacred. Our earth is sacred.

Our bodies are sacred.

Dawn

REFLECTION

Dawn's son shared the details of our telephone conversation and his mother's letter with his family, telling me that everyone felt their mother's presence in the beauty of her words. Months later, I opened my email to find this note from her daughter:

It is a rainy day here in Alaska and I find myself sitting in a cafe with enough built up courage and energy to finally write to you. It has been months since my brother forwarded me your email. It was shocking, raw, and intense when it first came.

There have been moments throughout the spring and summer when I wanted to reach out, to learn of your book's progress and just say "hi" and "thank you for reaching out." And yet, I wasn't ready to do it in those moments when this email exchange crept into my mind. With leaves turning and dark skies nestling us in for hibernation, I'm feeling more space to be able to make contact.

I have so many questions. First and foremost, I do want to express my gratitude and appreciation for the way you contacted our family with such special messages. I'm happy that my brother remained open to speak with you and then relay this information to me.

Everything you have written down and shared exudes the spirit of our sweet radiant mother, Mumma Habash (Dawn), at her finest, with vibrancy and big energy that really hits home. It's quite clear and obvious to those of us who knew her.

I love her message and if you'd come to know her while she was here, you would've quickly learned that speaking with her was always a triangular conversation between healthy relationships, food, and physical wellness. And then for her spirit to weave in the transformative information on the movement of life to death was utterly captivating.

To be able to understand and speak about death, I believe it will help us in understanding life more. I am grateful for this sacred knowledge to be passed onto us through her and others. Thank you for sharing with us, and the world!

Yasmine

FRANK

SURRENDERING CONTROL

"We have control over our choices—to fly or to flee."

— Frank

While food shopping one January afternoon, I ran into Betsy, a woman I had met at a fundraising event in our town weeks before. She confided to me that a mutual friend of ours had shared with her that I had a gift for connecting with departed loved ones. Betsy had lost her husband Frank three years earlier. We chatted, then exchanged phone numbers, and went about our day.

When I awoke the next morning, the white snow covering the trees and fence in my back yard reminded me of an artist's sketch. The soft beauty of the quiet scene seemed to whisper to me to be still, breathe deeply, and rest in my thoughts. I was reminded of Betsy. Speaking with her the day before, I could feel her longing for her husband, as if a blanket of snow was covering her heart to keep precious memories frozen in time forever. That morning, I felt Frank's energy soaring; the song "Wind Beneath My Wings" played in my ear. I felt his gratitude, love, and honor for his wife, his hero, reminding me how love transcends our physical realm.

Upon sharing this with Beth, she was shown Frank sitting upon a stationary bicycle, peddling, but not getting traction. We were receiving the information that Frank was good at overcoming obstacles, but he could not beat his cancer diagnosis.

There was a gentleness about him, rooted in a strong sense of conviction. We both received the image of an army-green jacket. When I later inquired whether Frank had been in the military, Betsy explained that he had served in the U.S. Army in Korea. Frank then went on to show Beth a windshield, as if symbolizing his desire to protect his loved ones by shielding them from the pain and sorrow of watching him battle cancer. Frank had a lightness about him, a good sense of humor, and his energy was calm and reassuring as he channeled this letter to Beth within twenty-four hours.

FRANK'S LETTER (JANUARY 2019)

Dear Betsy,

Do not mistake my illness, the ravages it took upon my body and my battle, for one that I was not meant to fight. The war that raged in my body was not really a war with the physical, but the mental. To ensure that surrender was possible, I had to give up that control. No matter how hard I fought, or how hard I tried, I could not win that war. I was unprepared for the humbling that we all have to endure. We are no match for God and for what life has in store for us. Nobody is, really. We think we are. We plan. We dream. We try and predict.

It was important that I was able to protect my loved ones, but I could not protect them from what was beyond my control. It was the ultimate fate for me to succumb to something that brought us to a place we never imagined travelling.

But I am free now, to soar, to fly, and I have come home. I know it is still hard for my loved ones, as they are not flying above it all. But I want them to know that we all have a contract to fulfill—both with life and each other.

It is our free will, our choice to fulfill this contract, and not everyone will do so. I was to endure all that I did in order to help me surrender control. I will not lie. I was so glad to be free from the pain and it all. But I also feel proud of what I endured and what I survived. Yes, I survived.

I know you think of me as your hero, but you are my hero. You are the one who gave me the strength that I so needed. When my wheels were spinning and I just could not gain traction, you were there. I would not have been able to get through it all without you. Perhaps it is not what we go through, but who is there for us when we do that is important.

We had a contract —you and I, my dear. And I could not be prouder of you for enduring and suffering by my side, no matter what life brought our way. I did my best to protect you, but in the end, I had to leave first. If you can understand it, that is the way it was meant to be. For now, it is up to you be independent and live your life until we meet again. Not to dwell on what I endured but to celebrate what I survived. I am reminding you that I have survived. I am a survivor, in so many ways. And so are you. We all are.

Life is not easy. Even those whose life seems to have little challenge, who are filled with love and joy, have personal struggles. Some of our struggles are private, and nobody can see. Others look upon these people and think they have it all. It is just not true. It is just the human way to compare, and sometimes come up short, and other times, come out ahead.

Sometimes, our struggles are on a large scale and others become part of it. That can happen when a family member becomes ill, or addicted, or even when there is a manmade or natural disaster. These are all struggles and that is why we all came here.

For to struggle, to hold on tightly, is to know the human way. To surrender control is to know God's way.

(Beth is hearing the song, "My Way" by Frank Sinatra.)

Yes, I did it my way, but I also had to surrender my way for God's way. For my way is what we all have in mind when we live our life. We believe we have control and can plan our destiny. But we do not.

We have control over our choices—to fly or to flee. Perhaps free will is what occurs, if you think about the notion that we plan our life here on earth. In that sense, we have had a say. And yes, we can even change our contract, renegotiate while here. And we are in charge of that.

We have planned our illness, our accidents. Our losses. Our success and failures. We have planned it before we arrive, and then it is our job to get on to the plan or not. To fulfill our contracts or break them. It is also our job to separate and know when our contracts are up. When our time here on earth is complete, or when a relationship has run its course.

And if need be, we can renegotiate and change while here. We have that choice. We are always in charge of that. And so, it is fruitless to blame or to resort to revenge. The sooner we get on to our life's plan and surrender to what is, the less we spin our wheels or dig our heels into the ground.

We cannot prevent what we have chosen to experience any more than we can stop the flow of time while here on earth. It is always for our highest learning and growth, no matter how physically or emotionally painful.

There is no pay back here, only learning. No failure, only growth and success. Even if we change our mind, and do not or cannot fulfill our contracts here, there is no judgment, only the understanding of why that happened. Why we veered off course and perhaps never returned to our path.

Even that is something for us to learn for next time.

I know this is a lot. I am feeling the need to recap so that you understand, my love. That is part of who I am, to ensure your safety and security.

We must surrender our will. We all create our contracts before coming to earth and it is our job to fulfill these promises. We can also change our contracts while here on earth. Nothing that happens is by accident. We all have struggles— some are more obvious, others more personal.

If not to feel while on earth, if not to endure while on earth, if not to know pain and remorse while on earth, if not to feel loss and shame while on earth, then where? I ask.

My training earlier in life was to find the strength and understanding to prepare me for my final battle.

I waged the perfect war and one that taught me to give in to what I could not change, to let go of control, to fulfill my contract no matter how much I would not remember creating it.

You are the wind beneath my wings.

Until next time, you have my whole heart and my love. I am watching and loving you.

Frank

REFLECTION

On April 1, 2019, Frank's wife Betsy sent us her response to the words and content of her husband's Sacred Letter.

My connection with Frank through Berit and Beth was swift. I felt the words were his—the references to flying free (my husband was a glider pilot) and the surrender he had to eventually accept (especially as an athlete in life with his description of riding a bike without moving) were his explanation in words for what I already understood in Spirit. The way he spoke about us, and his love for me, were also his words. The emotion and confirmation I felt was overwhelming. Some of the message was broader than just a message to me and I have accepted that he may also be speaking beyond me. I have been reassured of Frank's presence around me and with me, by Frank, and that gives me peace.

Betsy

MICHAEL

FINDING GOD

"Sometimes God is obvious, as in miracles, and sometimes,
He rests just beyond our awareness."

— Michael

The brother-in-law of a dear friend, Michael, passed from cancer, leaving behind his fiancé and family. Michael had a gift for making each person feel special; he fully acknowledged them, creating a perfect moment where time stood still. With his easy-going, accepting nature, Michael could effortlessly transform a potentially volatile situation between people into peaceful unity. I felt that Zen-like Buddhist quality about him, a Christ consciousness, when I first connected with his spirit at his memorial, Michael reminded me of a wise saying by Lao-Tzu, the ancient Chinese philosopher: "A journey of a thousand miles must begin with a single step."

Beth felt Michael's energy, too, and he gave her the image of palm trees and family. When Beth shared this with me, she said that she sensed that something special was about to happen, though she was unsure as to exactly what that meant. Michael's family was amazed when I told them, as they were planning to travel to Florida that Christmas for a special reunion with Michael's teenage son.

The next day, Michael came center stage and channeled his message through Beth. Michael spoke of his search for God, reflecting on his thirty-plus years here on earth, where he had been raised in the Christian faith while also being attracted to the teachings of Buddhism and Taoism. He seemed to have come full circle in his spiritual journey, as the truths of the Western and Eastern traditions now overlapped; different paths, yet all leading to the One Great Universal Source for All That Is. His journey had brought him back to where he had started: Home with God.

MICHAEL'S LETTER (SEPTEMBER 2017)

Dear Father,

Do you remember how old you were when you first began believing in God? For me, it was about grasping hold of something outside myself—something or someone more capable, more powerful, more enlightened. That meant giving up control of everything—my thoughts, my actions, my mind, and my heart. And that is ok. But so many don't know how to do this—to trust, surrender, and live their lives without limitations.

I know there are some people who have lost their faith; their belief in God has diminished because of their frustrations and the problems that can so often be encased in religion. For some parts of religion have taken the amazingness of God and created an image for the human mind to grasp hold of. This is when religion can be about judgment, fear, and limiting beliefs. Act this way, and you will receive that. Don't do this and you will be punished. Follow these customs, these rituals—all that we have set out, and do this without question because that is tradition.

Religion is too often created by our conditioning, adhering to beliefs that may temporarily speak to our human mind, but can also be limiting, stagnating, and suffocating. This is why our numbers are dwindling within our younger generation, why our pews are remaining empty and many of our churches and temples are closing. But we can turn this around. For religion can also open the doorway to changing our perception and open our minds to all possibilities. Religion can help us to find connection, love ourselves and others, and help us to dwell within the possibility of a higher being.

As I stepped back from religion, I found myself burrowing a hole deep within my heart. I asked myself the hard questions about life, healing, love, and relationships. Seeking out the wonder of just what I am capable of, I temporarily lost God in order to find God again. And this occurred through questions. How do I open my heart to God and my mind to limitless possibilities? How can I find God inside of me and not out there somewhere? How can I open my mind to go beyond what I have been told, shown, or seen? How can I step into the world of God and live from this higher awareness, beyond what this physical world presents?

Endless searching often brings us back to where we started. It is simple, although our minds complicate it. We have all the answers, all the power inside of us. We give it away on a daily basis—we look outside ourselves to other people for healing, love, and day-to-day decisions. We seek solace in a material good, or the false notion that if we just had this object, sought out this achievement, we would be happy and at peace.

The key is to live in the world, not of it. To find peace is to dip our humanness within the delight of a warm meal or conversation, yet not to lose our self in someone else's need for power and control. It is not only seeing God in the running of water from our faucet, but in the miracles that only God can perform. It is connecting to God through our questions and prayers, yet not losing sight of what God gives us in return—unconditional love, miracles, and magic.

We can transcend the limitations of religions, seeking out what works for us, without throwing out the notion of God altogether. What has helped me, and I share this with you, is to begin by releasing all you have been taught about God and begin to feel what God truly is about for you.

To help you to see what God may be for you, I will explain what God is for me. Please know that whatever term we use for God—Jesus, Buddha, Allah, the Universe, or Our Higher Self—it does not matter. But it is important for me to know there is something out there working for my highest connection, a force beyond what our minds can know and a pathway to open our hearts. When I can feel, trust, and know it before I can see it, then when I do witness God stepping in to save a child, heal a body, provide an insight,

I am not surprised.

Nor do I think God has escaped from someone's heart or left someone behind to fend for him or herself when death or destruction occurs. For sometimes God is obvious, as in miracles, and sometimes, he rests just beyond our awareness, and time helps us to see all He does. Does this mean that God is not there when a child dies or when tragedy and hatred blind the eye? That is too easy an explanation for the darkness and evil upon this earth. That God has abandoned us when we need God most. Open your minds and look beyond the event, the spoken word, and find a way to rise above, to open your heart no matter what, and know that each person who has walked this earth has come here to do good. Something or someone has caused them to go awry, to stray, to forget, to succumb; but God is still in their hearts, often buried beneath their pain.

I have even found at times, God can test our faith, but that is to just help us become stronger and wiser within our choices and growth. I have found God. I have nodded and said yes that there is something at work out there, beyond myself. I have given myself over as I have lived my life in the awareness that I am not alone.

I know I have given you a tall order by asking you to move beyond our human created notion of a "father figure" and kick off the practicality of your upbringing. To discard the notion that we alone must control our every action and those around us with judgment in order to feel safe; that we need to be right in order to feel good about ourselves; that we do not have the power within us, given to us by God, and must seek it elsewhere; that we are not good enough, strong enough, loved enough.

To release our conditioning as if we are taking off an ill-fitting piece of clothing that is too itchy, small, and binding is our goal. Then we can free our arms to open them up to endless possibilities. We can look up to seek God but knowing that God is guiding us through the love in our hearts.

That does not mean God is absent. For God is in all our hearts and when we open ourselves up to the truth, we find ourselves listening to that higher knowing in how to live our lives on the path of worthiness and love. We know how to take care of our needs and to honor ourselves. We learn to navigate life and relationships with God as our guide and love as our mentor. We learn to open up to our power within ourselves as our soul guides us through another day, another hour, and the most auspicious of moments.

And it is those moments when we have peeled back the layers of conditioning, judgment, and powerlessness, we find God within our hearts. We do it in any way that we can. For some, that is to sit in a pew among fellow worshipers. For others, like me, it is to deepen the connection through nature, leading me to self-awareness, self-love, and self-guidance.

It doesn't matter how we find God. But to have a practice and commitment will ensure that God illuminates within our hearts and we find the unconditional love, magic, and miracles. Then we can see that it is God that stops a plane destined for failure from taking off or saves a boy from drowning long after he stops breathing. When hundreds of thousands gather in opposition to racism and hatred, we say thank you. When insight relieves our hearts of a burden of guilt that was never ours to endure, we say, Amen. And when our bodies heal miraculously, our hearts burst open in ecstasy and joy at the simple sound of the chirping of a bird, and we say, yes, of course, God was here.

Thank you, God, for stepping in, for guiding me down the path that enables me to remember all that is important and forget what is not necessary. Thank you, God, for reminding me how to love myself and forgive others. Thank you, God, for waiting patiently for my knowing to unfold and my truth to arise. Thank you, God, for opening my heart to unconditional love and my mind to endless possibilities! Thank you, God, for showing me all the miracles and magic that life brings.

Michael

MALLORY

UNMASKING FEAR

"Once we see fear for what it is,
we must extinguish it each and every time with love."

— Mallory

Beth came across Mallory's story while scrolling through local online news stories. Her heart sank when she read about what the middle-school girl had endured; she had been endlessly taunted and bullied, leaving her to feel there was no way out other than to take her own life. It was no coincidence that, at the time, Beth's son was also experiencing the tragic and far too common issue of bullying. Mallory's story resonated deeply with Beth, and each time her son was bullied, she felt Mallory saying, "Pay attention." This problem does not just go away on its own.

Action needed to be taken to protect Beth's son from the boy who was doing the bullying.

When Mallory's Sacred Letter came through, Beth and her husband were already very aware of the ongoing incidents of bullying at school and were involved in efforts to protect their son. Although met with resistance from the school, they were determined not to be dissuaded by opposition and fear. Sometimes standing up for what we know is the truth may not be pleasant. Mallory's Sacred Letter encourages us to move beyond fear and reach for the truth.

MALLORY'S LETTER (NOVEMBER 2018)

Dear Beth,

Please know the fear you are feeling is not yours. It was mine. I was too afraid to tell what I was really feeling. I was too afraid to let the adults in my life help. You have willingly opened yourself up, and so has your son, to bring this issue to light. This is such a common issue, not just with kids but also with adults. Bullying begins out of fear and it continues out of fear. Many see no way out, other than to unleash their fears upon others. Unknowingly, they are not helping themselves.

I am reminding you of a phrase you've heard before: "hurt people hurt people." You know this. Do you know how scary and what a helpless feeling it is to be bullied? But it is not just the bullying, but the process one needs to go through in order to remedy the problem. It appears that for your family, the problem has not been fixed, it has just been shuffled around. This happens more than you realize.

At one time, nobody was aware or knew what to do with bullying. Now, they are aware, but too afraid to take appropriate action. As a result, the one being bullied is left feeling helpless and unheard. Eventually, if this continues, it creates the "no other way out" scenario for the one being bullied, and taking one's life becomes the only perceived answer.

This is not just a child problem, or an adult problem. This is a world problem. Children bully children. Adults bully adults. World leaders bully world leaders. The stakes rise as do the ages of those involved. Weapons of mass destruction are just as much the means to unleash one's fear upon another as a child's teasing. Somehow it is believed that taking another one down will lift ourselves up. This could not be further from the truth.

Fear is at the base of all bullying.

Your family and your son have taken this on in order to help others. Do not become lost in what the end result will be. The lessons are in the minutia, the everyday occurrences. You are teaching your son how fear works and teaching the adults how it plays out in our world. I know I am repeating myself, but this is important. This is so much more than you. This reaches far and wide. How you are handling it winds up having a ripple effect, like a pebble tossed upon still waters. You did not willingly pick up the stone, but by not ignoring what is happening, you have tossed it in the water.

As you take in my fear, remember to let it go. I have just placed it inside of you so that you will understand how I feel, how your son feels, how everyone feels who is being bullied. It is an old feeling for you, and that is on purpose. For how would you know how to dispel it and answer your call to action if you have never experienced this yourself?

I see how you are beginning to understand. We all have a job to do and that is to reach beyond fear. To see how it plays out in our life, whether we are being bullied or our livelihood is threatened. It blinds us to the truth, and we find ourselves acting out of character, or more importantly, out of alignment with our ethical knowing.

Fear pushes us to forget our compassion, our humanness, and that we are all love. Fear covers our ears and our eyes. Fear cripples us. Fear causes us pain and suffering.

The way we remedy fear is through two steps. First, we must see it for what it is—the reason for all suffering and pain. The culprit behind the illness. It robs us of our true nature, creating a mask that we all hide behind.

Once we see fear for what it is, we must extinguish it each and every time with love. For fear cannot survive in an atmosphere of love. Love suffocates fear and each time we extinguish it with compassion over competition and support over hate, love wins.

Make no mistake, fear is relentless, and it will return time and again in other ways, through other paths. It will open every door that is left unlocked and make itself at home. It knows your weakness, so you must strengthen yourself from within. Compassion for yourself and others and speaking the truth will lock all doors to fear, leaving it at your doorstep.

We all unknowingly invite fear into our homes. Welcome it with a freshly cooked meal, and so often, we do not even know it has sat at our dinner table until we see all the dirty dishes. That is ok. Cleaning up the dishes is where we begin. Bathe yourself with love and the next time fear comes knocking, you will remember to lock the door. It is better to eat alone than to dine with fear.

We must band together so fear does not knock upon our neighbor's door. We must be nosy and see where fear is sneaking in through the cracks of their foundation. Where fear has created the cycle of abuse of children. For it is this child that repeats this action upon his classmate. This is how we come full circle.

We can find our connection with each other. We can choose love over hate, so that fear does not find a pathway into our homes and hearts. We can discover where fear is creating a block to love, and our thinking has gone awry. We can point the finger at fear and say, no! Not today, or tomorrow. Not ever.

Facing ourselves and where fear has entered our psyche is the first step. Replacing it with love is the last.

We can all reach beyond fear. We just need to take that first step towards each other and let love in.

Mallory

REFLECTION

I felt Mallory's spirit strongly beckoning me to write this reflection in response to her words, wise beyond her twelve earthly years, calling out bullying as an expression of fear. Rejecting hurtful words requires strength from within, and also knowing that one does not need to carry this burden alone.

This responsibility is on all of us, she tells us. Too many feel isolated as a result of the weight of shame they carry from being bullied. They are burdened with having to overcome what seems insurmountable, and don't know who to turn to. It takes courage for them to step up and break the silence. It takes all of us to speak up and act on behalf of those being bullied, to be vigilant about how others are being treated. We are our brothers' and sisters' keepers.

LOUISE

MENTORING THE SOUL

"To know myself as whole and complete
is to know perfect health."

— Louise

I remember my amazement when Beth described how Louise's spirit had come into her awareness. Beth was lying in bed, about to fall asleep, when she felt Louise standing beside her. It was spontaneous and unexpected, yet her appearance at that moment left no doubt as to who this spirit was. Louise had arrived just as we were sorting through the many Sacred Letters to decide which ones to use for this first book. She helped us to bring order to our collection by suggesting titles for the three sections. This marked the beginning of a very special mentoring relationship.

Louise seemed to have been following everything we were doing from afar before stepping forward to provide guidance with the organization of our book. By this time, we had begun to amass a treasure trove of profound messages from an ever-expanding circle of spiritual contacts.

Beth and I were familiar with this inspirational author, healer, and publishing legend. Louise had played a prominent role as a leader in the new health revolution focused on balancing the mind-body connection. For decades, she had offered hope to those suffering from physical diseases, since she had cured herself of cancer with the natural healing program she promoted in her book. Louise encouraged others to live a life of abundant health, success, and happiness, and championed the power of forgiveness, self-love, and affirmation.

Louise would become our welcome mentor, reminding us that despite humble beginnings, all was possible. Her presence was gentle and reassuring, yet persistent. We could feel her no-nonsense, get-to-it attitude, leaving little time for dilly-dallying when there were tasks to be completed.

At one point, we saw her polishing her nails, alluding to polishing the manuscript. Another time she was sipping a cup of tea and nodded in approval. Then, more recently, wearing a stylish wool suit and glasses, she helped us to organize a task. Louise returned often while we were putting this book together and she continues to be very present in our lives.Beth and I are eternally grateful for all of Louise's support and encouragement to see this book through to completion. Her candid message in this Sacred Letter reaffirms that those who have passed can continue to communicate and help so many.

LOUISE'S LETTER (SEPTEMBER 2017)

Dear Light Workers:

I know you do not fully believe that we can speak, or that I have come to you—and to that I say, why the heck not? Why would I not be able to speak to you? I can be with you and so many others all at the same time. I am here for you to take in what I say and give out what you write. My life on earth was dramatic, amazing, inspiring, crushing, incredible, humbling, and beautiful.

Every single life is beautiful. My purpose was to help people heal—through their bodies and through their minds and into their souls. That is your purpose too. We all have a purpose and sometimes we do get ill or sick or have a disease to bring us closer to our purpose, or to teach us something we cannot otherwise learn.

Death should be a celebration, a beginning, not an end. You are mystics that bring forth a new way of thinking to those that do not know or have yet to understand this new way of thinking. It is not difficult to get; it is just that most are not ready. They are caught up in a conditioning that keeps them stuck in a pattern.

So you want to know about the body. Miraculous healings are possible, but more so, for those who devote time and attention to caring for themselves, and the divine is the surest way to healing. If a miraculous healing occurs, it is because it is meant to occur for the individual's journey— to change them forever. But most need to devote time and attention to connect, go inward, and find the voice of their souls that is so often buried beneath the negative judgments from another. It takes effort. To combat conditioning takes commitment.

Our souls are pure and unadulterated. They are beautiful and all knowing. They are subtle and gentle. They are brave and secure. They are a pathway into joy and peace.

I have devoted my life to healing, but it began with me. Healing my body. I had to do it blindly, not knowing where it would take me. We do not know where our path goes, but we must have faith and follow our soul, that voice, that intuition, that gentle urging that encourages us to look and go beyond what we see and know. To melt into what we feel and know is the pathway to our soul.

My passing, like my life, was unexpected but welcome. I lived a long life and it was time. I laid the groundwork for so many and I have nothing more to do there, but lots here. I am excited to release my body, but grateful for all it taught me while I was incarnated on earth.

I am sitting with Wayne Dyer, and I am playing golf, and I am conversing with so many. I am also speaking with you.

And I want to talk with you a little about food, the importance of nutrition in healing the body. It will take spiritual work or self-introspection to the next level. To eat foods that are alive and nurturing helps one to feel alive and well.

Too often, we indulge in the opposite—food that sits on shelves and has chemicals. Our bodies do not want this. Our bodies want whole foods. This does not mean depriving ourselves, as there are so many pure, wholesome foods that are also delicious. It is not a prison sentence to eat these foods, but a way into freedom and lightness of being.

You must listen to your body. It has all the answers. It has a myriad of ideas and notions. If we all just understood how our bodies are here to help us. That it is not about what is on the outside. What shows on the outside is just a metaphor for what is going on inside of us, within our hearts and souls. Our bodies are trying to teach us, tell us, help us to become aware—to slow down, nurture, speak up, honor, love, cherish, devote, welcome ourselves in ways we have not been doing.

If our emotions are inroads into our desires and where we need to hear, our bodies are paths into our souls—it is one step beyond our emotions. Our emotions are there to get our attention, so we know where to delve in, go deeper. But to listen to our souls, we must strip away our conditioning, the outer layer, and then we can hear and know the truth. It does not happen overnight, but neither does illness.

If we could only understand the simple notion that getting sick is not bad but a blessing. That fear is not to be avoided but is the portal into all we have ever wanted. That we are put in uncomfortable situations so that we can grow and evolve. Getting all that we want and never having any pain only keeps us small. Rising above, going through, welcoming all we feel is the ticket to freedom and peace, joy, and bliss.

As I always said while in body, to know myself as whole and complete is to know perfect health. For when we leave pieces of our souls, go against ourselves, hide our truth, judge and blame, we become shattered and broken. Rest, nurturing, nutrition, self-reflection, connection with divinity, hearing the voice of our soul—that is the road back to wholeness, back to ourselves, back to peace, joy, and love.

Nobody on earth is beyond love. It is our God given right

to love and be loved. To feel peace and joy. When we are not feeling these things, we need not ask why. We just must see where we have ventured away from ourselves. Look to our feelings to bring us back. This will be the key.

Do not hide under false pretenses that all is ok when it is not. Be honest with all our feelings—anger and jealousy are just as important as happiness and joy. They all are temporary, but our souls are permanent. So do not avoid the moment, our feelings, what is the truth. It will allow you to hear your soul and this will set you free.

I am free now, not in my body. But I have always been free. There is no difference for me. I chose to heal my body while still in it. You can too. There is a way out of pain, misery, and contempt. There always is.

You just need to make the choice. It is yours now and forever. It is all of ours. The choice to be free, to honor and love. The choice to be honest and truthful, to have integrity with ourselves. The choice to hear and follow our soul, for it knows the path of our purpose. The choice to release caring what others think and stay true to ourselves.

This is the path to salvation. This is the way to love. This is the road to love and light. Through suffering may salvation come. We are one and all.

For now,

Louise

DEAR READER

The love and insights that we received from the souls who sent us the Sacred Letters gave us a new perspective for living a life beyond fear. We are grateful to have received their words. We had to trust that we were being guided by something far greater than ourselves. In each of the messages, we recognized a precious piece of our own selves. Their stories were our stories. And we felt a wondrous connection, reaffirming the truth of our immortality, that our souls live on.

Living a life beyond fear is a journey that starts with a moment of recognition when you know without question that you are never alone. The angels and spirits are right there beside us to help us find our way back to our true self, back home. The spirits of these Sacred Letters give us a superhero cape to break free of self-doubt and fear, knowing that anything is possible. We all have the ability to tap into the unseen realm to feel boundless love and support and receive exactly what we need. The challenge is to open our minds, feel through our hearts and connect with all there is.

We hope that you can feel the healing power of these letters, the grace that transformed us from skeptics into believers, allowing us to honor our calling as spiritual messengers.

We have witnessed how these messages have changed the lives of many people with whom we have shared them.

In our journey together we are still learning, just like you. We are humbled and awed by what we have received from Spirit and excited about what we have yet to discover. We'll continue connecting with the many souls waiting to share their "love letters" with us—so that we can share them with you.

Thank you for joining us on this sacred journey!

Beth Mund and Berit Stover

Visit us online at www.thesacredletters.com

QUESTIONS FOR REFLECTION

The following questions are designed to help you integrate the messages of the Sacred Letters into your daily life. This list can be used for your private reflection and self-study, shared with a friend, or used for a group or book club discussion.

Would you consider yourself a spiritual person? Why or why not?

Have the Sacred Letters in this book changed the way you think or feel?

Do you believe in life after death? Why or why not?

Which part of this book did you relate to most strongly?
Explain why.

       Opening the Mind?

       Feeling Through the Heart?

       Connecting with All There Is?

Which of the voices/spirits in the Sacred Letters resonated with
you the most, and why?

Which message(s) did you find the most challenging to accept
as truth?

What are your greatest fears? How does your fear and self-doubt shape the way you view yourself and the decisions you make?

Has this book changed your awareness of fear and how you perceive the world around you?

Have you made, or can you see yourself making, actual changes in your life because of the way you now view fear?

Do you or a loved one suffer from addiction? If so, has the Sacred Letter on addiction changed how you view this issue?

Have these letters affected how you view grieving?

If you have lost a loved one, have you been able to go within and feel the connection with that spirit in a new way?

Are you aware of a Presence around you reminding you of that loved one?

Did you feel a connection with the authors' experiences?

What are your spiritual gifts? Have you shared them with anyone?

What are you grateful for in this moment?

How do you connect with your inner self?

    Through meditation?

    Walks in nature?

    Quiet times?

    Through creative expression?

Do you have a practice to go within and connect with Spirit?

What can you do at this moment to expand your imagination and visualize your divine self?

What steps can you take in your everyday life to make this your new reality?

ACKNOWLEDGMENTS

This book would not have been possible without the spirits who honored us with their words and presence. We are deeply grateful for their generosity and patience in sharing their profound messages from the afterlife. We are humbled by the family members of these spirits who, despite their grief, gave us permission to share the stories of their loved ones and use their names in our letters. We are eternally blessed by all those who guided us in bringing forth these Sacred Letters to help people live a life beyond fear.

We feel blessed by all of the love and support from our families. Without them, the Sacred Letters would not have been possible.

I am grateful to my husband Mitchel for his unconditional love, always believing in me. My children Gabrielle, Lia, and Drew, who brighten my world; and baby Griffen, whose tiny footsteps never touched the earth but whose spirit opened my heart.

Special thanks to my family and friends for opening their hearts while encouraging me to honor my gifts, knowing the truth of who I am. —Beth Mund

I am grateful to my husband Gregory for his unwavering love, and to our twins, Austin and Sarah, whose own incredible gifts have expanded my world. I am forever grateful to my parents, Edith and Dolf, who always told me that anything was possible. I am grateful to my beloved sisters Kristin, Margrit, and Erika for sharing an extraordinary eternal bond of sisterhood, and for providing intuitive insights and guidance for presenting these letters. —Berit Stover

We are grateful to our editor Kendra Langeteig of Edge-Wise Publishing for her insightful editorial support and guidance. We give thanks to our graphic designer Dan Yaeger of Nu-Image for capturing the magic of the Sacred Letters on our book cover and website. Special thanks to Francine Catanese, Ellen Crowe, Christine Fritsch, Garry Gewast, Sally Keighley, Elizabeth MacPherson, and Suz Stone; thank you for graciously reading our manuscript and providing valuable feedback as we finalized our book.

ABOUT THE AUTHORS

BETH MUND's essays have been featured in Elephant Journal, Grown and Flown, A Room of Her Own, Living the Second Act, Blunt Mommy, and the anthology The Walker Within as well as in her inspirational blog, Alternative Perspective. Beth has a B.S. in Psychology from George Washington University and a M.S. in Psychology from Nova Southeastern University. She is certified in Reiki and Wellness Coaching. Beth lives in New Jersey with her husband, three children, and two dogs. She is the co-author of *Living Beyond Fear.*

BERIT STOVER managed the Japan-America Student Conference, one of the first bilateral educational and cultural university student exchange programs between the U.S.A. and Japan, before pursuing a career in the international transportation logistics industry. She holds a B.A. in International Relations from Mount Holyoke College and has served on multiple boards for international and local non-profit organizations. Berit lives in New Jersey with her husband and twins. She is the co-author of *Living Beyond Fear.*